Sticky Fingers, Sticky Minds:

Quick Reads for Helping Kids Thrive
From the Parent Powerline

By BECKY CERLING POWERS
Veteran Homeschool Grandma

CANAAN HOME COMMUNICATIONS
Vinton, Texas

Copyright © 2020 by Becky Cerling Powers

All rights reserved.

No part of this book may be used or reproduced
in any manner whatsoever without written consent
from the publisher, except for brief quotations for reviews.
For further information, write Canaan Home Communications,
170 Hemley Road, Vinton, TX 79821
or email at: becky@beckypowers.com

First Edition 10 9 8 7 6 5 4 3 2

LIBRARY OF CONGRESS CATALOGING-IN-PUBLICATION DATA

Names: Powers, Becky Cerling, author
Title: Sticky fingers, sticky minds: quick reads for helping kids thrive/
Becky Cerling Powers
Other titles: The Parent Powerline
Description: First edition. Vinton, Texas: Canaan Home Communications

Library of Congress Control Number: 2020946043
ISBN 978-0-9672134-0-8 Sticky Fingers, Sticky Minds:
quick reads for helping kids thrive

Cover and interior designed by Kathy McInnis, kathy@ivyleafdesigns.net

Sticky Fingers, Sticky Minds:
Quick Reads for Helping Kids Thrive
From the Parent Powerline

BECKY CERLING POWERS

CANAAN HOME COMMUNICATIONS
Vinton, Texas

Dedicated to my parents,

Bob and Laura Jane Cerling

ENDORSEMENTS

Note: *Sticky Fingers, Sticky Minds* is a compilation of a few of the parenting columns Becky Powers wrote during the 1990s and early 2000s for the *El Paso Times, Clinton Herald,* and *El Paso Scene.* Here are comments from those readers plus a mom who is reading them in manuscript form now, today:

As a parent of two young children, I read Becky Powers' tips on parenting for creative techniques dealing with the habits and chores all parents face, like putting the kids to bed or teaching them to clean up after themselves. Her advice has made it easier to avoid common pitfalls and roadblocks. I credit Becky with teaching me how to be a more creative communicator and enrich my relationship with my kids. Her column is the most useful material on parenting I've seen.
  Eddie Holland
  Business Manager, Cinco Puntos Press

Becky Powers' parenting column quickly became "must" reading for parents after its introduction to the Clinton Herald *some five years ago. Its simple down-to-earth approach suggests activities which help children learn while having fun with their parents; tips parents (and grandparents) can use to combat the 'What can we do now's?' familiar to all families. I've seldom seen a column gain a following as quickly.*
  Bill Baker
  Clinton, Iowa
  Retired editor of the *Clinton Herald*
  (40 years in the news business, 25 years at the Herald)

Becky Powers wrote a column for the El Paso Times *for about 10 years, and even though I am not a parent, I always read her column* because it was insightful, interesting and entertaining.

She knows how to motivate children and parents to be interested in learning and discovering the world around them. She has innovative ways of getting kids to read, get interested in math and science and learn about the arts.

She writes in a way that is sophisticated, but not over people's heads, and she always has fresh ideas. I was always surprised at the subject matter in her columns. She would write about subjects I had never even considered being discussed in parenting. And after reading them, I would think about how I could use her advice in my dealings with children as president of a saddle club, in which most of the members are youngsters.

Laurie Muller
News Editor
El Paso Times

Dear Becky,

Just a note to tell you how meaningful your columns are to me and our daughters. Our daughters have inquired if you have any books published on helpful tips in success with kids.

Jean Barco
P.S. I cut out and mail all your columns
to our daughter in Houston!

Dear Mrs. Powers:

Thank you for your wonderful column in the El Paso Times. The tips you share about interacting with children add up to worthwhile reading. You write with clarity. You entertain. Your weekly features are Sunday morning delights.

As a writer I appreciate your easy-to-read style. As a grandmother and a crafter I look forward to your ideas, especially those involving things usually found around the house. You prove time and time again that youngsters can be entertained even in families whose budgets are strained to the limit.

I regret one thing, though: If only I'd had the tips in your Bedtime Battles column – way back in the '60s when we were raising our five nap-fighting sons. Nevertheless, I can now benefit from your advice which is easily adapted to times I spend with our granddaughters.

Any parent, grandparent, Child Care professional or babysitter could certainly learn much from your helpful features. I'd also recommend that anyone who is studying Child Development would gain much understanding through your direction of love, patience and sincerity in relationships with youngsters.

Again, many thanks for your insights.

Cordially,

Mary Ann Herman

I feel the absence of your column from the "El Paso Times." Your practical advice and suggestions of activities truly does help kids succeed. As a mother of three, I have often found new approaches to parenting difficulties, academic helps, as well as ideas for creating family memories in your column. Over the years, I've clipped and filed several for posterity. I've witnessed clippings of your column at a home schooler's co-op bulletin board and a preschool bulletin board as well. My daughter's kindergarten teacher sent home copies of your column on hundred's number board to assist our little ones with counting, and math when they are older. Your column. "Helping Kids Succeed" was something we could put into action right away!

Sincerely,

Karen M. Ward

Dear Ms. Powers:

Your weekly column is one of the parts of the Times that I make a point of reading (even when I'm a week behind and am "catching up" by reading only the comics...and your column). Keep up the great work!

Sincerely,

Janet M. Crowe

El Paso, TX

Dear Mrs. Powers,

I find your column helpful because I am a speech pathologist in the schools and love children. The suggestions are very useful with the children I see who stutter. The common sense parenting ideas are really great and beneficial for planning ahead, getting organized for the next day, good eating habits – just to name a few.

I am usually able to just copy your articles and hand them to parents after discussing them. Most of the time, I have to remind the parents of the necessity of following the advice several times. Change comes slowly.

I am sure that I have missed some of your columns – do you happen to have them all in a binder or somewhere I could get copies of them? I have saved many of them. Thank you for such an outstanding column.

Sincerely,
Carolyn Kolpin, M.S., CCC-SLP
El Paso, TX

Dear Becky,

Your last three columns have been extra special to me.

Thanks for helping me think more deeply. I've no doubts: my granddaughters will benefit!

Regards,
Lynne Baldwin
El Paso, TX

Becky-

I thought you may enjoy this! (picture enclosed of two recently adopted daughters). Thank you for your note of encouragement when we requested your article on kids' cooking skills. I have a binder with plastic pocket pages, which many of your articles find their way into. You are a great help to new parents like us! Keep up the good work!

Love,
Debby Manion
Clinton, Iowa

Dear Ms. Powers,

My name is Jan Holland, and I teach kindergarten at Dr. Green (EPISD). I read your article about not rushing children to read and providing a literature rich environment. If possible, could you please fax a copy of the article to my husband – (name and fax phone number). I agree strongly with your comments and would love a copy for some of my students' parents.

Thanks,
Jan Holland
El Paso, TX

Most parents don't need a long lecture on parenting – sometimes just a few well-timed words of advice can make the difference. Becky Powers' monthly "How to be a Better Parent" column in El Paso Scene *offers exactly that: one tip for each day of the week. Her pointers on parenting combine common sense and deep spiritual values that are sure to produce stronger, sounder families. Every mother and father – and their children – will be enriched by this column.*

Randy Limbird
Editor
El Paso Scene

I saw your column twice in the El Paso Scene, *so I cut it out both times and sent it to a young mother I know. The column is very gentle, very encouraging and very practical also. I think it is lovely. Usually I only pick up the* El Paso Scene *occasionally, but now that I know that column is in the Scene, I will definitely be picking it up every month. I will get it because of that column.*

Susan Anchondo
Continuing education teacher

As family editor of the Clinton Herald, *I strongly recommend this column. I look forward to reading it and editing it each week.*

As a mother, I only wish her columns had been available when I was raising my child. I could have used her fresh, patient approach to child rearing. I especially enjoy her suggestions for making routine household chores a pleasant activity instead of a war of wills.

Powers offers gentle advice in dealing with children in all aspects of their rearing. Her columns are full of warm memories of a family growing together and learning from each other. After reading several columns, the reader almost feels she is a part of her family.

Penny Smith
Family Editor
Clinton Herald
Clinton, Iowa

Hi Becky!

I read through the manuscript you gave me. The book will give the reader a vision for what a homeschool/healthy home can look like—one bite at a time.

People right now need a voice of reason pointing out what real learning is. They need reassurance that the daily things matter and that there's more that needs to be taught than what can be learned in front of a computer screen at virtual school. If (and most likely when) that method fails—especially with little kids—these ideas are a good and needed back up.

Probably my biggest issue in taking the plunge to homeschool was having the courage to do it. These stories ought to give the readers confidence that they can pull it off.

Even if they don't choose to homeschool, the principles for healthy homes and real learning still apply and will be helpful to any parent.

Jill Bell
Homeschool mom

Table of Contents

Introduction 1
Parents: Sculptors or Gardeners? 5
Give Your Children Sticky Minds 9
Minimum Maintenance 12
Why Play with the Kids? 15
Emotional Safety 18
Reading to Babies 22
Conversing With Your Kids 25
Preparing to Raise Teens 29
Let Kids Cure Their Own Boredom 32
Teaching Children to Cook 36
Major Transitions 38
Helping Kids Love Reading 41
Figuring Out Learning Styles 44
Give Kids Reasons to Learn Math 48
The Balances of Raising Kids 51
Homestyle Secrets of the Learning Process 54
Preschool at Home 57
Tire 'Em Out 61
Troubles with Math? 64
Training vs. Setting Kids Up 67
Working With – not Against – Life Seasons 70
And Speaking of Seasons 73
Taking Walks 74
Preventing Parent Burnout 77
Biology and Late Blooming Readers 79
The Lazy Parent's Secret 83

Kids in Touch with Math 86
Music Enriches Family Life 89
Nature Hikes and Expeditions 92
Hooray for Mother Goose! 95
Educate with an "I Love You" 98
Training Kids to do Housework 100
In Praise of Naps 103
Organize Your Child's Bedroom 106
Push "Easy" Books for Reading Fluency 109
Modifying Games for Children 112
Attention Deficit Disorder 115
Learning in the Doctor's Waiting Room 119
Making the Most out of Bedtime 121
Bedtime Battles 124
Teach Your Child to Read 127
Money Lessons by Age 130
Money Management Basics for Kids 133
Best Toys are Simple Ones 135
Using the 100 Chart for Math 138
Treasure Hunts 141
Turn Kids on to the Past 143
Toddlers Helping 145
Kids Writing 149
Healthy Snacks 153
Science at Home 156
Lighten Up! 159
Use Rhymes to Teach Essentials 161
Fun with Magnets 164
Teaching Jessica History 167
Education, Western Culture and the Bible 170
Tackle Problems Head On 174

Introduction

One day back in 1983, when our daughter Jessica was 9 years old, I was relaxing with a book at the park after her soccer practice while she played on the swings with one of her teammates.

"Do you have Atari?" I overheard her teammate ask.

"No, we don't have a TV," she said.

He was instantly sympathetic. "You mean your parents won't let you watch TV?"

"No," she said patiently. "I mean we don't *HAVE* a TV."

The boy stopped his swing and stared at her. "Gosh!" he exclaimed. "What do you *DO*?"

I giggled into my book.

"We read," Jessica said. "We do lots of things."

When our children were small, my husband Dennis asked me if we could go without TV while he was trying to write his doctoral thesis. He felt he was too addicted to the tube to write a thesis while working full time. I agreed because I didn't like the way TV took over our schedule and interfered with communication in our marriage.

Looking back, now that our children are grown, Dennis and I agree that that decision was one of the smartest moves we made as parents. We were no longer tempted to use the TV as a babysitter, which forced everybody to use their time more creatively.

Without TV, the family talked more, played more, and read more. The kids invented more games, created more projects, imagined more elaborate ideas, explored more territory, experimented with more concepts, and read more books to themselves and to the rest of us. And when they did watch a movie or TV, they enjoyed it more.

"I have never seen children have so much fun with a TV show," a friend told me once. She had offered to let our kids see "Ichabod Crane" at her house while we were chaperoning a church youth party. "Your children literally fell down on the floor and rolled around laughing," she said.

A couple years after we moved to El Paso, in 1985, I wrote to the feature editor of the *El Paso Times*, telling her the story of how our TV-less daughter shocked her soccer mate at the park. I asked if the Times would be interested in having me write a weekly summer-time column about TV-free activities for kids and families to enjoy during summer break. That letter began a 15-year relationship with the *Times*, writing family features and, eventually two weekly parenting columns as well as, one year, editing a daily story column for a year-long community writing project.

The *El Paso Times* required my primary column, "Helping Kids Succeed," to be 750 words or less, so I tried to pack the ideas into short pieces that were quick to read but, hopefully, thought-provoking enough to be long-lasting in effect.

I was in the middle of homeschooling our three children when I wrote them, so I was tutoring subjects at several grade levels while managing meals and housework. It gave me lots to write about. For one thing, homeschooling taught me to do one-to-one tutoring, which is a different method of teaching than classroom teaching but is the kind of teaching that parents and grandparents helping children with homework must do at home. When I began writing about how children develop math skills or how to help children love reading, people began telling me that their child's teacher photocopied one of my columns and handed it out to all her students' parents. Or they said that their child's principal posted one of my columns on a bulletin board for parents to read. Homeschool parents told me they collected all my columns in a binder.

Readers told me they looked forward to reading the column, like sitting down for a cup of a tea with an understanding friend to gain perspective on their family issues. "You'll never know," one mom told me, "what a difference your column on emotional safety made in our family."

She said that one of her sons constantly belittled his little brother and teased him in mean ways because, he reasoned, "At school the other kids are going to do that. He has to learn how to take it." Reading the column about keeping home as a safe retreat for every family member gave this mom and her husband the word-pictures they needed to counter their son's argument and insist on a family standard of kindness.

Once when I was visiting my sister 800 miles away in Houston, she took me to dinner and introduced me to a circle of her friends, including a young mother who was astonished to realize that I was the writer of the newspaper columns her grandparents in El Paso mailed her every week. That's when I learned that grandparents and great-grandparents were sharing the columns with their adult children and grandchildren.

And some people even told me they read the column regularly even though they did not themselves have children.

That was two decades ago and more. But as I talk with my young mom friends, teachers, fellow grandparents, and others, I find that certain issues keep coming up and again, issues that I once covered in a parenting column. So I find myself making copies of old columns to give people, and later I learn that they helped: a toddler who wouldn't sit still for reading a book with mom now loves being read to, young teens start reading books at night instead of watching TV, a mom reports a more peaceful relationship with her daughter...

Since these parenting columns are still helpful to people, I decided to update and republish a selection of them in a book. (I also republish them as blog posts at www.beckypowers.com)

The best way to read this book, I think, is to keep it handy for short, quiet moments – read a chapter during your bathroom break, your waiting spell at youth soccer practice, or your wind-down time before bed.

I decided not to order the chapters in the book by age or topic. Although some chapters touch on concerns for specific age groups, most of them concern multi-age issues. And while parents may be worried about a very specific topic—like teaching a child to do chores—they may find the key to family change in a chapter dealing with another topic altogether – like figuring out learning styles or like training children versus setting them up. So whether people read the chapters straight through from beginning to end or dip into the topics here and there, I hope they find those nuggets of insight they need to help the children they love grow healthy and meet their full potential.

Parents: Sculptors or Gardeners?

When our first baby was born, I had the great good fortune to be friends with Ruth, a writer who was a dozen years older than me. Ruth had three big assets for me—she delighted in her four children, she was going through a mid-life crisis, and she stuttered.

Ruth's practical approach and obvious enjoyment of her kids provided me with a wonderful role model. And because she was going through a mid-life crisis, Ruth was re-evaluating her life and close relationships. And because Ruth stuttered, she did more thinking than talking. When she finally decided to say something, her words were brief but powerful. Her pithy observations gave me lots to mull over.

Ruth's parenting metaphor

Ruth was the youngest of 13 children, so she had been able to watch quite a few of her brothers and sisters raise their families before she started raising hers. She said she noticed that her siblings viewed their children as lumps of clay to be molded and formed. But she felt that was the wrong mental image.

Instead, she said, she viewed her family as a mystery garden from God and her four children as little sprouts in the garden. Her task as a mother was first, to figure out what kind of plant each child was. (Was she tending a rose bush or an apple tree? A field of onions or a grape vine?) Her second task was to provide the very best growing conditions for that kind of plant.

Molding or nurturing?

So when I saw parents trying to mold their child into a particular future ("My son is going to be a high school football star," or "My daughter is going to be a nurse") I realized it was like going into a garden and saying, "I'm going to turn this plant into a pecan tree." That only works if the plant is already a pecan tree.

If the sprout is really a raspberry bush, parents will be frustrated when, instead of a tall tree with hard, crunchy pecans, they get a prickly bush with soft berries they are unprepared to do anything with. They'll be disappointed with their crop of sweet, luscious berries. And they'll say stupid things to their raspberry bush like "Why don't you produce pecans like your brother?" Instead of providing a trellis for their little climbing rose, parents with a molding mindset will punish her for not staying in place.

So Ruth's metaphor helped shape my parenting.

What my dad had to say

Perhaps Ruth's observation made extra good sense to me because, although my parents used different words to express it, I now realize they raised their six children with the same philosophy. And I saw what healthy relationships they had with all their adult children.

"What should parents do to have a good relationship with their kids?" I asked my dad once when I was interviewing him for a Father's Day parenting column.

He said, "First it's important to have lots of shared activities." So my parents did what they loved and included us children. Sometimes we were interested in doing those things, and sometimes weren't. But either way, sharing a great variety of activities with us made it possible for my parents to do what Dad said was the second important thing: observe your children closely to discover who they really are – what their individual interests and talents are. Dad called this recognizing your child's natural bent. "Parents," he said, "need to do whatever they can to help their children follow their natural bent."

Sharing activities and encouraging special interests

So my parents gardened, and we kids helped bring in the harvest. Mom showed us how to help her make homemade jellies, jams, and applesauce from harvested fruit. Mom liked to bake, so we all learned to bake cookies and cakes. She liked to sew, so she taught my sister and me to hem our skirts, make doll clothes and eventually use the sewing machine. Dad liked woodworking, but none of my brothers showed any interest until they were adults themselves.

My sister liked art and house design, so Dad encouraged her to take a drafting class in high school even though in those days, drafting was considered a class for boys only. My brothers liked sports, so Dad practiced with them and my parents cheered them at their games. They liked science, so Mom and Dad took them to science museums and my dad took them around to his construction sites and told them about engineering problems he had to solve.

Our whole family loved music. We sang in the car on long drives and our parents stretched their budget to give us music lessons. Often after supper Dad gathered us all up to sing while he played his mandolin, I played piano, one brother played bass fiddle and the other brothers played guitar.

Mom and Dad encouraged my writing

They encouraged our interests. I liked to write, so they praised me by telling me specifically what they liked about things I wrote. For example, Mom might say, "I especially like the way you described the dog in your essay. It gave me a vivid picture and made me laugh." They encouraged me to write to foreign pen pals, and my mom and I wrote to each other when I went to summer camp. I kept a journal, too, and my parents made my sister and brothers respect my privacy and keep my journal private.

In high school they encouraged me to join the high school newspaper staff and write for the school's creative writing anthology. When a local weekly newspaper invited four students, each from a different local suburban high school, to publish a monthly column about what was happening at their school, my teacher got me the job writing the column about my high school. My parents cut out and saved my columns, showing me their interest in my work.

By my senior year in high school, I knew I wanted to go to college.

But I had no idea what to choose for a major. I liked history and literature and psychology. What should I choose? Then my mom saw an article in the newspaper about a brand-new journalism scholarship, and she told me I should apply for it. I was positive I wouldn't get it, but my mom wanted me to apply, so I did, using the newspaper columns my parents had clipped for the required samples of my writing. And I won the scholarship. So that's why I majored in journalism.

My parents understood me much better than I understood myself. By steering me toward journalism, they gave me the push I needed to get the right kind of university training for the kind of writer I am.

Six kids, six different, fulfilling careers

My folks used the same loving approach with all six of their children. Today my sister is a well-known artist in Houston with her work on display in the Houston airport. I am a journalist, columnist, and author. One of my brothers is a geology professor who is in the National Academy of Sciences and made discoveries that people use in crime labs to solve murder cases. Another brother is a clinical psychologist. My next brother designs computer chips and helped send a spaceship to the moon. And my youngest brother is an English professor. Six different kids, six different professions, all of us enjoying our work and our families.

Give Your Children Sticky Minds

I once read about a school district that tried a reading experiment with two groups of kindergartners. (This was in the days before No Child Left Behind, when local schools had the freedom to figure out for themselves what and how to teach and when to teach it.) The district gave the first group a lot of formal reading instruction and gave the second group hands-on science.

While the first group memorized the alphabet and sounded out simple words, the second group played with magnets, grew plants, melted ice cubes and learned about animals. Although teachers read to the "science" group and encouraged them to look at books and pictures, they gave these 5-year-olds no formal reading lessons.

By third grade the "science" children's reading scores were much higher than the "reading" children's scores. Their vocabularies and thinking skills were more advanced, and they could understand higher-level topics than the first group of children.

Why did the kids who weren't pushed to read early do better long term?

My husband and I have discussed this subject, and Dennis calls his explanation "The Velcro Theory of Learning."

Velcro fasteners, like the ones on children's shoes, have two parts. One side is full of teeny hooks, and the other side is full of teeny loops. When the two come together, thousands of hooks grasp thousands of loops, making a strong connection to keep the shoes on.

The contents of a good book are like Velcro loops, and a child's life experiences produce, inside his mind, something like Velcro hooks. The better the book, the more learning loops it has. The more varied a child's experience, the more learning hooks his mind develops for grasping those learning loops.

Working with a child's internal development clock

There is an optimum time when each particular child is ready to learn to read, usually between the ages of 6 to 9. All children, however, are ready to learn about the world around them.

In the school district's experiment, the "reading" group of children spent their time learning skills that were very hard for them developmentally at that time but that would become fairly easy for them to pick up a few months or years later. The "science" group of children spent that same time developing learning hooks.

Later, when the children's reading material become demanding at the third-grade level, the "science" group of children had a rich supply of learning hooks to grasp the new material firmly. The "reading" group had missed out.

Seeing the issue for myself

Years after reading about this experiment, I had an opportunity to see for myself the results of pushing children into reading tasks before their optimal readiness time. About 15 years ago, I was working as a teaching artist under a special grant, coming to a public school once a week to teach students in kindergarten through third grade and in special education to compose their own poetry. Using what I'd learned as a homeschool mom, I worked with kids at whatever learning level I found them, and the students all became very excited about making up poetry.

I shared an office with the reading specialist. We often chatted and one day she told me that she and the staff could not figure out why, year after year, the school's fifth graders seemed to give up on learning to read better.

"I think I know why," I said. "When I go into the kindergarten classes, the kindergarten teachers are telling me how conflicted they feel because the state teaching requirements make them push the kindergartners into learning skills that they are developmentally too immature to manage. It starts in kindergarten, the state teaching requirements demand more and more, the kids get pushed before most of them ready year after year, and finally by fifth grade, they are burnt out."

Here are a few tips for parents who want to nourish their children's love of learning:

- **Nurture your children.**

    Love them with your eyes, your touch, your words, your focused attention; provide healthy routines and sound discipline; draw them alongside you in your work and leisure activities; talk to them, listen to them, encourage their special interests.

- **Provide quality toys** that stimulate the imagination and help develop motor skills. Examples: blocks; building sets like Legos and Tinkertoys; sturdy cars, trucks, and trains; dolls and stuffed animals; puppets; puzzles; play dough, modeling clay and other art materials.

- **Take them on trips.**

    Go to museums, parks, libraries, theaters and concert halls, construction sites, fairs and fiestas, ranches, farms and factories.

- **Give your children an appreciation for reading.**

    Let them see you reading, and start reading them picture books when they are babies. Keep reading to them even after they can read for themselves.

- **Limit screen time.**

    Spend the time instead playing, working, talking, listening, creating, reading, thinking or inventing ways to avoid boredom.

Minimum Maintenance

How did your household cope with the 2020 Covid-19 lockdown? If you run your household on the Crash Crisis system, like I did when our three children were small, then with children unexpectedly home all day, every day, your home probably unraveled into a giant mess.

The Neglect-and-then-Catch-Up Cycle

The Crash Crisis system could also be called the Neglect-for-a-Good-Cause-System. I would spend a couple days on a special project, like making costumes for a children's musical, and then spend the next week fighting depression while trying to dig out of a disaster zone getting the household back on track.

Fortunately, before we began our 12-year adventure home schooling our children, I read *Totally Organized* by Bonnie McCullough, and learned to use McCullough's Minimum Maintenance (MM) system.

Keeping Up is Easier than Catching Up

The heart of the system is recognizing that "keeping up is easier than catching up." "Every house has a minimum daily requirement to keep it running smoothly," McCullough explained. Once you know which jobs must be done and which can be skipped, you need to accept your home's minimum requirement and see that it gets done. You don't have to do it all yourself, but someone in the household (usually you) must oversee the process.

Minimum Maintenance

For most families, the minimum daily requirement includes
- keeping up with laundry (have a regular place for people to

deposit dirty clothes; regular times to wash, dry, and sort clothes; and a way to return clothes to their owners before they get scattered. Children, depending on their age, can be taught to handle part of the laundry responsibility: for example, sorting and folding clean clothes).
- meals and meal cleanup (Our children took turns washing, drying, and putting away dishes. I oversaw clean-up, planned and cooked meals, but I also taught the children to cook. *(See "Teaching Kids to Cook")*
- keeping down the accumulation of clutter

The Focused Five-Minute Pick Up

For me, the heart of MM is McCullough's clutter solution: spending a focused five minutes tidying each room in the house (10 or 15 minutes in the kitchen) before leaving the house or starting any projects.

McCullough recommends that you use a timer and wear an apron or shirt with pockets. Start by picking up the biggest items first, and then work down to the smaller items that can be collected in a basket or pockets.

Just focus and do it

It's amazing how much work you can accomplish in five minutes. "Work fast and don't clean too deeply," McCullough says. "When you see jobs that need doing, jot them down on a project list for later, during cleaning time."

"Never feel so defeated by a tornado-struck room that needs several hours work that you don't do anything at all," she warns. "Just a few minutes in the room will keep it from getting worse."

The First Impression Principle

Begin your pick-up routine by keeping in mind the "First Impression Principle," McCullough suggests. "This means when you enter a building, if the first impression is one of neatness, you assume the whole building is clean. Most people don't notice smudges on a windowsill, they notice clutter." So, decide what a caller at your door sees first, and start by picking up that area first.

Training children to do daily focused pick-ups

This simple routine made a huge difference for me. In our home, with three school-aged children home all day, I gave each child the job of doing a focused five-minute pick up of their bedroom plus two other rooms (for example, both bathrooms) before starting school lessons. (Tidying the kitchen counted as two rooms.) That way we started lessons in a tidy house instead of trying to work in a mess. When we left the house early for a field trip, it felt good to walk in the door later to a tidy living room.

Don't expect the house to stay picked up all day

Of course we had plenty of lapses, and the house could get badly cluttered during the day, because everyone was home most of the time. But MM taught me that when my house felt out of control, I could get fast results and feel much better if I focused on it for even 30 minutes. And if the kids pitched in, the whole house could look dramatically better in only 10 or 15 minutes.

This pick-up time can be modified according to individual preferences and needs. You can set the timer for five minutes to work room by room or set the timer for 30 minutes and run all over the house picking up. If you have small children interrupting, you can do it in five-minute bites.

Houses do need cleaning. You can't give that up entirely. But throughout the year you can make what you have cleaned stay looking nice longer. And as long as you keep up with your minimum essentials (laundry, meals, and tidying), you can put your house "on hold" for quite a while in order to take time for special projects or get through a crisis like 2020's Covid-19 lockdown.

Why Play With the Kids?

When Karyn Henley and her husband play card games with their two teenage sons, the family often finds themselves in the middle of a lively conversation. "Suddenly someone says, 'Whose turn is it?'" Henley said. Then the family realizes that they have been talking for ten minutes, and they've lost track of where they are in the game.

"Playing with children is important for parents," Henley said, "because it helps make good communication possible."

How play builds communication

"When I talk about play in my workshops for parents," she said, "I emphasize that the first principle of communication is listening, and one of the catalysts for listening is play. Play becomes a format. While you're playing it's a prime time to listen to your child."

Henley is the creator of many teaching resources, including a best seller, *The Beginner's Bible.* She gives Child Sensitive Teaching seminars to parents and educators.

"When I talk about play that builds communication, I'm not talking about the parent having the idea and saying, 'Let's go play this,'" Henley explained. "Instead, it's asking 'What do you want to do?' It's joining in on the child's play."

"If a young child wants to crawl around on the floor and be a dog, you get down, too," she said. "With older children, the play changes. Instead of getting down on the floor, you play badminton or shoot baskets. It's still a format for communication."

Play builds trust and relieves stress

"Playing also builds trust and strengthens relationships," Henley said. "A bonding goes on when you're doing something together, for work as well as play."

"And play can actually be a great stress reliever for parents," Henley said. "Once you get into the playing, it is very therapeutic. It has an unwinding effect. You leave your cares behind for a while."

"When your children are preschoolers and you're running here and there, you feel this is going to last forever and all you want is a break," she said. "But really the time goes so fast, that soon you're looking back on it. And the chance (to build trust and communication with children) isn't there." So, play helps you enjoy your children during the short time you have them with you.

Play also helps establish a child's sense of self-worth.

"I'll never forget a letter I read once from a woman whose husband works with troubled teens," Henley said. "She said they all had been told in words or actions, 'I don't want you around.' They all felt worthless, the letter said, and when children feel worthless, they act worthless."

This woman's husband found out that there was one effective way to help these troubled teens, and that was spending time with them. That worked because saying and acting like you want to spend time with children gives them the message that they are worthwhile.

Some parents don't know how to play

Many parents feel inhibited about playing with their children because they were told not to play, that playing is childish and not for adults.

The first step for overcoming that inability to play is to realize that those messages are untrue, Henley said. "The first step is realizing that play is important and worth your time to do it."

The next step, she said, is to make yourself available for play. "Just sit down with your child when she's playing and observe. Young children have a way of drawing you into their play because it's so natural to them. If you're just sitting there, they'll hand you a teacup and say, 'I'll pour you some tea,' and include you in their little game."

Let children teach you how to play while they are still young

Being honest about your discomfort also helps, Henley said. "Whatever your children's age, you can ask for help. You can say, 'My mom and dad told me play wasn't good. They never played with me. I don't know how to play.'"

"Most parents who feel uncomfortable with playing would be surprised what that (honesty) would do and how much their child would reach out and help them," she said.

"It gets harder as children get older," Henley said, "so it's better to start when they're young."

Emotional Safety

"I can't allow you to talk that way to anyone in this house," I remember telling one of our young guests years ago after I heard him belittling our daughter.

"You see, this is a safe house," I explained. "You can come here and be safe. I won't allow anyone here to hurt you deliberately or call you names or put you down. But if it's going to be safe for you, it has to be safe for everybody. So you can't do those things either. I will not allow you to destroy the safety of this house."

A few years later that boy moved in with us for a couple weeks during a crisis in his family. He needed our home to be his safe retreat more than either of us could have guessed that day I corrected him.

We all need a safe retreat, a place where we can relax without fear of attack. Home should be that safe place, but establishing an emotionally safe home takes thought, diligence, and self-discipline.

Here are a few ways for people to make their home a safe retreat:

- **Guard your tongue.**

    Belittling comments, name calling, mockery and put downs are all taboo because they tear people down instead of building them up. My mother used to tell us children, "You don't hear your father or me talk that way to each other, so you can't either." Adults must control their own tongues before they can expect children to learn to do it.

    When parents slip up, using words to belittle or attack family members, they need to apologize. This gives children a good model for dealing with their own passionate or thoughtless outbursts.

- **Ban videos and TV programs that base humor on insults and put downs.**

    These situation comedies teach children the lie that it's "cool" to use humor to belittle other people. The truth is that belittling people makes them avoid you, and it destroys your ability to form trusting relationships.

- **Avoid shaming or humiliating children in front of others.**

    Whenever possible, correct children in private. Adults resent a boss who chews them out in front of everybody instead of drawing them aside for a private rebuke. A child's dignity should be protected in the same way.

- **Respect children's privacy.**

    As children develop a sense of modesty (usually around age 7 or 8), allow them to dress and bathe in private. Knock before entering older children's rooms (try counting to 10 to wait for a reply before assuming no one is in). Don't read diaries or personal mail without permission.

    It's also important to try to provide a place where a child can be alone with his or her thoughts. Solitude is vital for emotional health, and some children need more of it than others.

- **Respect children's personal property.**

    Some parents figure that anything that belongs to their children is really theirs, so they can borrow it without permission, lend it out, and generally do as they please with it. But respect is a two-way street. If you want your children to learn to respect your property, you must respect theirs and insist that siblings respect it, too.

    This should take some careful thought. You can't allow children to take advantage of this by claiming ownership of privileges. For example, children's bedrooms are not their own personal property because someone else is paying for it. Parents pay the rent or mortgage, so they can make rules about how their property is treated. A bedroom is a privilege not a gift, and children cannot demand that parents stay out and never inspect their rooms.

- **Listen actively.**

    Give your children time blocks of focused, undivided attention. Let them know you are paying attention by looking directly into their eyes and by responding to their words and feelings. Draw them out by repeating back to them what they begin to communicate: "Boy, that really made you upset, didn't it?"

    Children will be more willing to listen to what you have to say about a subject after they are certain that you have really listened to and understood their viewpoint.

- **Encourage your children.**

    Notice what they do right and say something positive about it. Recognize and praise the small steps they take on the way to achievement.

- **Use common courtesy.**

    Watch your tone of voice, and develop the habit of saying "please" and "thank you" instead of snapping commands. Greet children pleasantly when they get up in the morning or return home after an absence. Say good-bye when they leave the house.

- **Teach the Golden Rule by word and example.**

    Treat children the way you want to be treated yourself and help them think through the process of treating each family member the way they themselves like to be treated.

    We as adults can start thinking of our kids as just an extension of ourselves...like a third arm. "I need this work done; therefore, my third arm should do it."

    In our marriage, if someone asks me if I my husband will do something for them – even something very simple – I say I'll check with him. I don't volunteer him for the job because it's disrespectful to make decisions for another adult.

    Parents have to make a lot of decisions for their children, but as they grow into teens, the kids need to make more and more decisions for themselves. I was fortunate that my parents recognized that. I had a lot of babysitting clients, but my parents never took on a babysitting job for me if someone called when

I wasn't home. They took down the information and said they'd tell me to call the client back. Likewise, although my parents did ask me to babysit my younger siblings for them *gratis*, if I had a paying babysitting job, they didn't make me give up my paid work to do unpaid work for them.

They used the Golden Rule.

Reading to Babies

All the experts tell parents, "If you want your children to become good readers, you should read to them often."

"But, what if my toddlers won't sit still when I try to read to them?" some parents ask. "What if they lose interest and wander off before I finish the story? Or before I turn the page?"

Read-less reading

That's where read-less reading comes in. Introducing children to the joys of reading actually begins with first enjoying books without reading the words.

The process is simple. You talk your way through the book. First you label and describe the pictures. Then you begin telling the story in your own words and pointing out details in the pictures.

Moving into "real" reading

As your children's vocabulary and attention span develop, you ask questions and let them tell you about the pictures. At the same time you move gently into "real" reading—you read bits and pieces of the text until your children become ready to listen to whole stories just the way they are written. From there, you gradually move along to stories with fewer pictures.

Eventually, a grade-school child trained by this process will happily sit still for a half hour or more to hear a rousing good children's classic without pictures.

Read-less reading is an easy skill to pick up. You just need to know your child and then think up things he or she will like. The possibilities are as endless as the differences in children's personalities and interests.

Here are a few ideas to try:

- **Labeling pictures and imitating sounds.**

    In general, babies and toddlers like simple pictures of people and anything that makes noise. They like their "stories" with action and sound effects.

    At this age, wordless picture books are the best place to begin, for parents as much as children. (Since there is no text, you have to learn to make up your own words.) Also, because a baby or toddler's attention span is brief, you usually point out only one thing about a picture. Example: "There's the baby. Let's kiss the baby. (Kiss picture, turn page) Here's the clown. The clown has two funny shoes. (Tap each shoe) One, two. (Next page) Here's a cow. The cow says MOOO. (Turn page.)"

- **Expanding vocabulary.**

    As a child's vocabulary increases, you can begin asking questions about parts of the picture, like "Where's the doggie's tail?"

    Preschoolers, whose vocabularies are exploding, often delight in learning specialized terminology. A favorite book for many preschoolers is *Richard Scarry's Best Word Book Ever.* Each page illustrates and labels many items in categories—types of boats, kinds of work machines, different animals at the zoo.

    You can flip through the pages and teach children correct terms for the subjects that most interest them. (You don't have to look at every page of a book any more than you have to read every word on a page.)

- **Repeating words, ideas, story lines.**

    Children find security in routine—repeated activities, familiar pictures, stories that remain the same. They learn vocabulary, speech patterns, counting, thinking skills and many other things through repetition.

- **Playing silly games.**

    Sometimes when parents get tired of reading the same old story many times, they can try reading the familiar words wrong, as a joke. Then their children correct them, and the reading time turns into a silly game: "Well, let's see, the name of this story is 'Little Brown Pear Loses His Toes.'" "No, no, Daddy! (giggle, giggle) It's 'Little Brown Bear Loses His Clothes.'"

- **Playing question games**.

    Parents can also encourage their children to observe closely through question games, like *"How Many?"*—a game for children who are learning to count. "How many dogs in this picture? How many balloons? How many cars?"

    "Where is it?" is another good game. "I see a mouse in this picture. Where is it?" Question games are not intended to be tests, but a way to praise children and build their sense of accomplishment: "Good for you! You found the mouse."

    "What if..." is an imagination stretcher: (Looking at a zoo scene) "What if we could get one of these animals for a pet, for Daddy's birthday present? Which would you pick? Why would Daddy like the elephant? Where would we keep it? What would we feed it?"

- **Just having fun**.

    It's fun to turn these games around, too, and let children ask parents the questions.

Read-less reading is more than just a way to keep children interested in books and lengthen their attention span. It builds thinking skills, and it develops observation skills children will need in order to learn how to read themselves later on.

Most of all, it's fun.

Conversing With Your Kids

The 2020 Covid-19 pandemic kept children home from school all over the world. And of course, parents and grandparents worried that their children and grandchildren would get behind in school.

Actually, there are many, very simple things that parents and grandparents can do to help pre-schoolers and school age children with their need to develop academic skills whether or not the children are able to attend school.

One of the most important is this: from the time they are babies, talk with them (NOT talk *at* them, talk *with* them). This is because for young children to do well in school – and in life! – they need lots of opportunities to develop language skills through back-and-forth conversations.

Talking in the car

If you turn off the radio in the car or the TV at home, there are lots of opportunities to talk. I was driving with 5-year-old Jacob one rainy morning on the way to running errands. When we came to a traffice light, I pumped the brakes to keep from slipping on the wet pavement.

"Why are you doing that?" Jacob asked.

I explained that when the surface of the road gets wet, it's slippery. So I needed to use a special way to stop, to avoid an accident. "It works the same way at home," I said. "Do you remember yesterday, when we washed the kitchen floor, and you ran on it when it was wet, and you fell down?"

He remembered. We talked about that, and then we talked about the importance of cleaning up spills right away – especially spills on the floor. People can slip on them and get hurt.

Talking about expectations before going into the store

Our discussion on household safety was finishing just as we drove up to the shoe store. Jacob and I talked about what to expect in the store and how I expected him to behave – a quick and natural lesson in social skills. Later, as we left the store, I complimented Jacob on his good behavior.

Talking in the grocery store

After that we drove to the store for groceries. "Look!" Jacob said, pointing to a huge number above one of the aisles. "Around and back /On the railroad track."

"Yep, that's a 2," I said. ("Around and back" was a chant we were using to help Jacob learn how to make the number 2). Then Jacob found other numbers he recognized and read them for me. He read some of the letters he recognized on labels, too.

Talking about manners

When I spied a lady at a booth giving out food samples, I coached Jacob on what to say: "You can ask her, 'Please, may I have a sample?' and then when she gives you one, remember to say 'Thank you.'"

He remembered, so I praised him. "You used very good manners, Jacob."

Talking about new words

Later, in the checkout line, Jacob pointed to an Emergency Exit sign and asked, "What does that say?" I told him, and then we talked about what "exit" means, what an "emergency" is, and what kinds of things might happen in a big store that would cause people to need to use an emergency exit.

Jacob was fascinated with the idea of emergencies. On our way home from the store, he brought up the subject again. So most of the way home we talked about different kinds of emergencies and good ways people use to handle those situations.

Daily conversing enhances self-esteem and develops language skill

These kinds of daily, natural conversations do many things for a growing child. First, warm responsiveness from adults builds a child's sense of self-worth, while at the same time, it encourages him to keep trying to learn the complicated skill of communicating well.

Second, conversing with children on subjects that interest them helps children learn their language. Anyone who tries to learn a foreign language as an adult knows how important it is to hear the language spoken properly and to have practice speaking it to an attentive, sympathetic audience in order to become fluent. In the same way, conversing with children lets them hear their language spoken properly, it gives them vocabulary and phrases for expressing many kinds of ideas, and it offers them a chance to practice using language themselves.

Daily conversing lays the foundation for reading and writing

For the first ten years or so of a child's life, according to noted educator John Holt, developing skill and interest in talking lays a foundation for learning to write well and read well in school.

"A child who does not talk will not have many things that he wants to say, and hence will not know what to write about," Holt wrote. "When he does try to express his thoughts, he finds it hard, because he has had so little practice in putting words together."

"Lack of skill in conversation is also likely to make poor readers, at least of many kinds of writing..." Holt said. "The good reader enters into an active dialogue with the writer. He converses with him, even argues with him. The bad reader reads passively; the words do not engage his mind...In courses like Math or Science, in which one must often follow instructions, turn other people's words into action, the inarticulate child often finds that he can't do it."

Being a good communicator also helps children to make friends and get along well socially.

Conversing with children takes a lot of time and effort, but it is one of the essentials of being a good parent, grandparent or special friend to a child.

Preparing to Raise Teens

I used to sit in my junior high English class and think, *When I grow up, I never want to teach junior high students. People this age are horrible.* And later, when I had children of my own, I dreaded the day when they would turn into adolescents.

But when the day arrived, I was pleasantly surprised. I enjoyed that time – at least, most of it. There were a few rough spots, of course. But looking back over it all, our three children's adolescent years were easier than their preschool years, when we were laying the foundation for what was to come.

How toddlers can prepare you to raise teenagers

One of the secrets to surviving, appreciating and even enjoying a child's adolescent years is this: you have to grow up yourself first, to prepare. Our children used to embarrass me into growing up. I'd see our two-year-old pitch a temper tantrum and realize that I had pitched a fit just like that (not as dramatic, not as loud, not as public, but still, just like that) only the day before.

By definition, small children are childish—that is, they are impatient, self-centered and unrealistic. (Just spend half a day with any toddler for an on-site demonstration.) And in varying degrees, most of us parents start out our parenting with these same characteristics of immaturity.

What immaturity looks like

We get irritated because we don't want to wait for things, or for other people. Or we get angry because we want to stay comfortable, and we're being called on to tend a need instead. Or we explode when our children don't meet our unrealistic expectations that they "should" be doing things that are actually beyond their stage of development, or they "should" behave radically differently from other children their same age.

Our own impatience, selfishness and foolishness tell us that we must work some more on growing up ourselves before we can guide a child through the maturing process. But how do we change?

We get impatient trying to learn patience. We're too wrapped up in ourselves to remember that we're supposed to be learning to think about others. And we'd rather be mad about our disappointed expectations than face reality. Meanwhile our failures keep hurting our children.

It is at this point that parents either give up through despair or denial (more unreality) or else they use failure as a door to understanding and action.

What we all need most in order to truly mature

What failure can teach us, if we let it, is that our greatest need when we fail is for someone to love us anyway with no strings attached – despite our failure and despite our immaturity. We need unconditional love because we've just proved we can't meet the conditions for earned love. Yet, along with forgiveness for our failures, we also need the balance of a challenge to do better next time.

We need people who love us this way and who let us practice loving them that way, too – forgiving us and giving us practice forgiving them. (Getting chances to practice forgiving is never difficult as long as you're around other people.)

We need people who show us a better way to handle things – models and mentors. We need spiritual counselors, too, who can show us how to get the power to change. In short, we need to develop a good support system of other adults from family, church and community who will encourage us both to mature and to love unconditionally so we can be better parents. (Of course there are no perfect support systems. Most will also provide us with some bad examples, too – to show us what to avoid.)

What unconditional love is and is not

Learning to love our children unconditionally doesn't mean we like everything they do and let them do it. We can love them while hating their behavior in the same way we can love a friend while hating the cancer that is destroying her life. That means that even when we are making our child lose privileges for bad behavior, for example, we can still show affection, still giving loving eye contact, still say, "I love you no matter what."

Loving in a self-centered way means we show love only when our child does something to make us proud or happy. Conditional love seems easier than loving unconditionally – until it dead ends.

For children are love mirrors.

In his book *How to Really Love Your Teenager*, child psychologist Ross Campbell says that children can only reflect back the love their parents give them. If parents love unconditionally, children love back that way. And if parents show love only on condition, when they judge that their children have done something to deserve it, then children learn to love the same way. By adolescence, parents and children are stalemated because each party is withdrawing love and waiting for the other one to make the first move by doing something special to earn their love.

The special reward for unconditional love

Unconditional love, though, has a special reward for parents of teens (and this is true even though no parent loves unconditionally 100 per cent of the time). Adolescents have a strong drive to independence, and that drive requires lots of emotional fuel, Campbell says. The fuel teens prefer is unconditional love.

So when parents convince their children that they are a reasonably reliable source of unconditional love during the preteen years, their children will keep coming back to their parents to fill their emotional tanks when they are teens.

And during adolescence, that can make all the difference.

Let Kids Cure Their Own Boredom

I used to think it was my responsibility to keep our children entertained and occupied all the time. I wasn't a good mom, I thought, if my kids were bored.

After a while, though, I realized we were establishing a predictable dialogue pattern that went like this:

Them: *I'm bored, Mom. There's nothing to do.*
Me: *Why don't you go outside and build a fort?*
Them: *It's too hot outside.*
Me: *Then play Monopoly inside.*
Them: *No, I don't feel like it.*
Me: *How about making a treasure hunt?*
Them: *No, I don't want to.*
Etc. Etc. Etc.

Finally I realized that sometimes children are bored because they are too lazy to do anything about being bored. And besides that, our children had started believing it was Mom's job to think up ideas and their job to criticize the ideas.

So I changed tactics. When the children complained that there was nothing to do, I said, "Well, I'll tell you what to do. You just sit right down in that chair and *think* until you figure out something to do."

Who is responsible for what?

The situation changed quickly once I realized who was responsible for what. It is parents' responsibility to provide raw materials and a rich environment that stimulates and encourages creativity instead of stifling it. After that, it is children's responsibility to do something about their own boredom.

Here are a few tips on what parents need to do:
- **Provide examples of creativity.**

    Take the time to let children work alongside you when you cook, sew, garden, etc. Let them work on their project while you work on yours. Also, invite children to help come up with solutions to family problems like, "What can we do for Father's Day even though we have no money to spend?"

    Read and tell stories about creative people. Perhaps a relative was a good craftsman or invented a good solution to a problem. Biographies of inventors, explorers, and artists, as well as historical fiction like Little House on the Prairie, are also good sources for tales of creative people children can emulate.

- **Supply raw materials generously.**

    Keep a supply of dress up clothes, costumes, and hats for pretend play. Stash materials like empty juice cans in a sack to be recycled into art projects. Provide pens, pencils, crayons, paints, brushes, paper, paste, tape, scissors, modeling clay and other art supplies.

    Never restrict a child to one piece of paper! Children need to make many drawings at one sitting to improve their skills. Having to produce perfection on the first piece of paper blocks creativity.

- **Provide work space.**

    Try to keep a desk, table, or some other working surface available for projects, and store art supplies where children can take them out and use them independently as soon as they are old enough to be trusted with them. (Keep potentially dangerous materials out of reach of toddlers, however.) Children will be less apt to start projects if they have to wait for you to clear work space and get out all the supplies.

- **Provide inspiration.**

    Buy children's craft and activity books or check them out of the library. Keep them handy so children look at them and choose projects to try on their own.

- **Provide house rules.**

Creativity tends to be messy. Part of being a parent is teaching children how to prevent unnecessary messes ("Do your cutting over the wastebasket so the scraps fall in there instead of on the floor") and how to deal calmly and efficiently with inevitable messes ("Clean up spills with a rag from the box"). It's also a good idea to have children ask permission before they use messy art supplies like glue, paint, or glitter.

- **Limit "creativity robbers."**

TV, tight scheduling, heavy loads of structured assignments, sophisticated toys, and a ready supply of "easy money" all rob kids of the incentive to create.

- **Provide outlets for creativity.**

Encourage your children to use their special talents for practical purposes. Let your artist make the family chore charts, design birthday cards, and decorate the house for birthdays and special holidays. Budding actors can give puppet shows, read aloud dramatically to younger brothers and sisters, or make tapes and videotapes to send Grandma and Grandpa. Aspiring writers can keep a family journal, compose poems for the artist's birthday cards, or write a family newsletter. An aspiring carpenter can make toys, build bookshelves, and put together "assembly required" furniture and toys.

- **Have patience with first efforts.**

Criticism (especially criticism of first attempts) withers creativity. Children improve with practice. You can always find something good to say about even the clumsiest first attempt at a new skill: "You sure used a lot of pretty colors that time," or "What an interesting idea. I would never have thought of that."

- **Provide lots of encouragement.**

Display children's art projects where people can see them. Express admiration for their efforts. Save and file their best efforts. Find instructors for children who want to develop a special talent.

Creativity is a latent ability in all children. Parents can do a lot to help their children develop and use their unique combinations of creative capability.

Teaching Children to Cook

Our children were about 15, 12, and 10 when I decided to stop making cookies and other homemade desserts so I could watch my weight. "I eat too much of that stuff when it's around," I told the family.

None of them complained. They just started baking goodies themselves when they got hungry for sweets – all of them, including Dad. So I found myself in a family of cooks, and I just had to learn to keep my hands out of the cookie jar when they filled it.

In retrospect, I think this happened because Dennis and I had encouraged our children to learn the basics of cooking from the time they were small and eager to "help." We realized that cooking is one of those essential skills children need if they're going to make it on their own when they leave home. So cooking lessons need to be a natural part of growing up.

Here are a few tips for the teaching process:

- **Start them young.**

    Children often begin to show an interest in helping cook at age 2 or 3. Let them help by dumping measured ingredients into the mix and licking spoons and beaters. Many 4- and 5-year-olds can learn to crack eggs, too.

    Elementary-age children can read recipes aloud as their reading skills improve and they can learn to measure ingredients. An extra benefit: Measuring ingredients is one of the best ways children learn to grasp the concept of fractions.

- **Expect spills.**

    Everyone spills something sometime. Children spill more than adults because they are less experienced and less coordinated.

When children spill, it's an opportunity for parents to teach them what to do with an accident. Show children where the rags are kept and demonstrate the clean up process. Next time there's a spill, remind the child in a matter-of-fact way where the rags are kept and tell him to fetch a rag. Unless a child is deliberately being destructive or goofing off, spills should be treated calmly, as a natural part of life, without scolding or punishment.

- **Know when to refuse cooking lessons.**

    Older children who have developed good cooking skills can be a great help to parents who are in a hurry or under stress, but serious accidents can happen if small, inexperienced cooks are allowed underfoot in the kitchen when people are working under pressure. So weekends may be a better time for cooking lessons than weekdays.

- **Build up gradually to simple recipes.**

    After children learn to read recipes and measure, they can begin putting together simple recipes, first under supervision and then on their own. When I found a recipe easy enough for the children to prepare solo, I wrote simple directions for it in a notebook that we kept handy in a kitchen cupboard. Once in a while I assigned a child the task of making a simple entree or dessert by themselves for a family meal. Children need lots of praise from Mom and Dad when they achieve this milestone. As children's skills improve, they can tackle harder and harder recipes. Our children were baking and selling bread to a couple neighbors by junior high age.

Children will need to eat all their lives. Teaching them how to prepare food for themselves and others is one of the essential tasks of good parenting.

Major Transitions

I was a confused bride.

My husband Dennis and I started our married life in Munich, Germany, where he was stationed with the army. For me it was a bewildering mixture of wonderful and horrible. Married housing on the military base was unavailable, but that was OK. We wanted to experience another culture. We were excited to have the chance to live in a German neighborhood, to try out the local food, and to explore the country.

It was exciting...but it was also unfamiliar – even scary. I was afraid to go very far by myself away from the apartment. What if I got lost? There were no cell phones then. If I wanted to phone my husband for help, I had to use a public pay phone. But the pay phone instructions were in German, and I didn't know enough German to understand them.

Lonely and unfamiliar

It was lonely, too, being so far away from my family and friends. While my husband worked long hours, I was isolated in a German neighborhood where I couldn't speak to my neighbors. And where I didn't understand the customs, like bringing a basket to the grocery store instead of expecting the store to give me a plastic sack.

Culture shock hit hard.

Missing single life

Marriage shock hit hard, too. I was used to being independent, living and working where I chose, managing my own schedule, paying bills with money I earned myself. Suddenly every aspect of my life depended on the work schedule, salary, and choices of somebody else.

I didn't want to tell Dennis that I missed my independence. He'd be hurt. So I felt guilty and disloyal and tried not to think about it.

Transition to a new life

Actually, in marrying Dennis and moving to Germany, my gains far outweighed my losses. My transition to married life and our cross-cultural adventure would have been easier if I known enough to *admit* the value of what I had lost, so I could move on. Running away from admitting my losses just kept me confused longer.

Like most people, I thought of grieving as something people only do when someone they love dies. Now I know that life is full of other kinds of losses that also must be acknowledged, mourned, and worked through. Our children shed their childhood and leave home for college and faraway jobs. Our parents age and lose their health. Dear friends get left behind when we move or start a new job. A pandemic like Covid-19 comes along upending people's schedules and lifestyles.

Steps of Transition

Every major transition involves losses. Most involve gains as well. Both the losses and the gains are real. Both need to be acknowledged, and our true feelings about both realities need to expressed, not denied. So instead of rushing on as if nothing important has changed, we need to acknowledge that something has ended. We can mourn an old way of life that we've lost, while at the same time celebrating and being grateful for new treasures in a life that has changed.

There are five steps for successfully making a major transition as individuals and families. As we put them into practice, we can help our children with their transitions, too. These steps are partially based on author Virginia Satir's suggestions in *The New Peoplemaking*.

- **Admit your loss.**

    Don't pretend nothing important has changed. Acknowledge that something has ended.

- **Grieve the loss.**

    Express it, put words to it, and even cry about it. Our feelings can be confusing. The week our daughter moved into a college dorm at age 16, I felt very proud of her. But I was a real grouch with the rest of the family. Finally one day when I blew up at my husband for asking me to run an extra errand, he asked, "Is this really about me asking you to run an errand on a busy day, or is it something deeper?" After a bit of resistance, I realized he was right. I wasn't upset about errands or schedules. *I missed my daughter!*

- **Recognizing clues.**

    Crying in frustration over my husband's request was unhelpful. Shedding tears over Jessica's move, though, helped me begin to accept the new situation. Crying helped when the tears were directed at the true source of my grief. Then I could also recognize and truly give thanks for all the positive aspects of the new situation: We made it! She graduated from homeschool early and went to college on a scholarship!

- **Recognize and give thanks for all the positive aspects of whatever has ended.**

    When I learned to grieve and give thanks at the same time, it brought me into balance. And then it became conceivable to recognize and acknowledge the potential in my life as a result of the change. My schedule freed up. My writing stretched in new directions. My daughter and I let go of our adult-child relationship and began moving into an adult to adult relationship.

- **Take action and move ahead into the new situation.**

    So I moved forward with gratitude, welcoming new possibilities and finding new opportunities to be thankful for.

Helping Kids Love Reading

Do you want your child to think clearly? Turn off the TV, read to your child and talk about what you read. And develop the habit yourself of reading good books and magazines to relax instead of turning on the TV. You'll think more clearly too.

Reading develops a different way of thinking from watching TV, according to Neil Postman in his book *Amusing Ourselves to Death*.

Reading trains the mind to analyze and reason. It stimulates the imagination and develops a long attention span. The fast-moving images on TV, however, encourage a short attention span and train the mind to jump around in a disjointed way and to respond emotionally instead of logically.

The way families across the nation encourage or discourage reading is closely related to the way children perform on school tests, according to a recent study conducted by the Educational Testing Service. Children in areas with a high percentage of families with three or more types of reading material at home scored dramatically better than children in areas with a high percentage who watched six hours or more of TV and did little reading.

Reading at home is the simplest way to enhance children's academic performance and to encourage children's intellectual development.

Here are a few tips collected from families who read at home:
- **Read aloud to your children no matter what their age or reading ability.**

    Bedtime is a good time to include reading aloud in the family routine. Be sure to talk about the stories and relate the characters and incidents to things that happen at home.

- **Encourage silent reading.**

    Some families give their school age children an early bedtime to allow them personal times for reading in bed.
- **Use the library.**

    Ask the librarian for help finding good books for children's particular interests, and use library reference materials like cookbooks, consumer magazines and travel guides to meet specific family needs, like finding good recipes, making important financial decisions and planning vacations. Here are four books that contain excellent lists of recommended books for children and teens: *Read Aloud Handbook* by Jim Trelease, *A Parent's Guide to Children's Reading,* by Nancy Larrick, *Honey for a Child's Heart*, by Gladys Hunt and *Honey for a Teen's Heart* by Gladys Hunt and Barbara Hampton.
- **Surround your children with good books of every kind.**

    Children need their own books as well as books on loan from the library. So for books to buy, check thrift stores, garage sales, catalogs, library sales, and new and secondhand bookstores.
- **Motivate your children to read by helping them find books that involve their special interests.**
- **Put a bookcase or bookshelf in your children's bedrooms.** They will be more apt to read for pleasure when books are handy.
- **Encourage children to read lots of books that are easy for them** instead of trying to push them on to harder and harder reading material. Reading lots of easy books helps a child become a fluent reader.
- **Daily practice reading aloud** is important for school age children. Encourage older children to read to their younger brothers and sisters. Let beginning readers read to anyone in the family with the patience to listen to and encourage them.
- **Take children of any age through a phonics program** if they have trouble reading.
- **Try shadow reading** with beginning readers or with jerky

readers who need to develop a smooth flow in their reading. Start with a book that is easy for that child. While you move your finger smoothly along under the line of print, read it aloud together with your child, as a duet. When he or she is moving along nicely, fade out for a few paragraphs (but keep your finger moving along smoothly) and then chime in again. Your moving finger will help train your child's eye to follow the print in a smooth flow.

- **Bring along a good book to read aloud to the family on camping trips,** long drives (if the reader is untroubled by motion sickness) and vacations.
- **Subscribe to good children's magazines.**
  Check out back issues at the library to find out which magazines your child likes best.
- **Record stories and let children listen to them** when you are driving in the car, during naps, and as they fall asleep at night. Clink a spoon against a glass whenever you turn the page while reading, so that later even pre-readers can follow along in the book as they listen to the audio story.
- **Hang a large world map in the kitchen** or some other accessible room. When a story is set in another country or is written by a foreign author, find that country on the map and talk about it.

Figuring Out Learning Styles

When our son Matt was a baby, he loved to feel soft things. He used to crawl into our closet and tug on my flannel nightgown until he yanked it down. Then he'd roll in it. While riding in his car seat, he would suck his thumb and stroke the hair of the brother or sister sitting next to him. He was into everything, too, and he was constantly on the go. When he cracked his front tooth, his dentist nicknamed him Crash.

Not surprisingly, Matt had trouble sitting still in school until we pulled him out to home school, and he had a frustrating time learning to read and write. By the time Matt was a teen, he had grown to be a gifted sculptor, a star athlete, a good reader and a terrible speller.

Like Matt, young children give clues about how they learn best. Parents who understand their children's learning style can work and communicate with them better, making it easier, for example, to teach chores.

Is this disobedience or inability?

A farmer once complained to psychologist Paul Welter, "My son is disobedient."

When Welter asked him to explain more specifically, the farmer said that his 12-year-old son did not do what he told him to do. At chore time, he gave his son three or four tasks. Sometimes the boy did a couple of them and skipped the others, and sometimes he did the tasks in reverse order.

When Welter arranged to have the boy tested, he found that the youngster had poor auditory sequential memory. This meant the boy was not deliberately choosing to "forget" his father's directions. Rather, he was unable to store and retrieve in his memory everything he heard.

This boy was a visual learner who remembered best what he saw, not what he heard. When the farmer began writing his instructions on a bulletin board for his son to read, the boy began doing his chores the way his father wanted.

There are three main kinds of learners:

- **Visual learners.**

    A visual baby wants to see what is going on. One family said their baby loves to be held, but if you restrict her field of vision by putting her up on your shoulder, she arches her back and lets you know that that is not where she wants to be. She is happy and content, though, if you hold her face outward so she can see everything you can see.

    Visual learners need to see what they are supposed to learn. They usually have an easier time in school than other learners because most curriculum is visual and most classroom teachers are visual learners themselves. These youngsters are usually "bookworms" who read lot and express themselves best through writing.

    Good educational materials for visual children are flash cards, matching games, puzzles, instruction books, charts, pictures, posters, wall strips, desk tapes, videos and simulation software, according to Mary Pride, author of *The Big Book of Home Learning: Vol. 1 Getting Started*.

    If these children have social or emotional problems, they respond well to reading books about other children coping with those same situations. Parents can give them material to read and then talk about together.

- **Auditory learners.**

    Auditory babies like to listen and experiment with sound. Once they learn to talk, they never seem to quit. Auditory kids literally have to hear themselves think.

    Good educational materials for these children, Pride said, are cassette tapes, educational songs and rhymes (like the

ABC song), and rhythm instruments. They learn best through verbal instructions from others or themselves. They will remember math facts and spelling words better by chanting them.

Providing an environment with good music will give these youngsters a lifelong love for music. They are good prospects for music lessons and instruction in foreign languages.

- **Touch/Movement (kinesthetic) learners.**

    These active babies get into everything. They learn best by touching and manipulating things. When they get older, they like to spend their free time building or making things. They are usually the fastest in a group to learn a new physical skill.

    These children tend to have the hardest time in school. They don't focus on visual or oral presentations, so they seem distractible. Besides, if they have to sit still, as children are expected to do in traditional classrooms, it takes all their energy and concentration to learn to do that. They have nothing left over for learning the subject matter.

    Hands-on learning is essential for these children. They need sandpaper letters, math manipulatives, long nature walks, model kits, and textured puzzles. "Be sure to have kinesthetic learners write BIG when they are first learning," Pride said. "Large muscle action zips through to the brain more easily than small, fine movements."

    Kinesthetic children may manage homework assignments better if they can stand (instead of sit) or march in place while working. When I noticed Matt getting jittery sitting at the kitchen table working on schoolwork, I'd tell him to put down his pencil and run around the house three times. Then he was able to focus on his work.

    One kinesthetic college student reported that his grades improved dramatically when he taped his textbook reading assignments and then listened to the tapes while jogging. When our son Matt went to college, he tried to take a P.E. or sculpting class every semester. Walking to campus and walking between classes helped him, too.

As teens and adults, kinesthetic people will often talk more readily if they are doing something active – going for a walk, driving, or working alongside a companion on a project.

"Few people only learn visually, or auditorially, or kinesthetically," Pride said. And some people learn well all three ways. But most people lean more to one style of learning than another. As parents, it helps to figure out our children's best way of learning and work with it instead of fighting it.

Give Kids Reasons to Learn Math

Why should any child want to learn math? Math is a lot of work, and children are practical. They aren't interested in going to the trouble to learn something hard unless they think it's something they need.

Adults are no different. I balked at learning to use a computer back in the late 1980s until my husband persuaded me that a word processing system would help me write the book I was working on. Later I became willing to learn even more about word processing systems because I needed to use my local newspaper's computer to write two weekly parenting columns.

Then I found that I needed to know how to set up spreadsheets to keep track of projects and finances. My growing need to do things that computers do well pushed me into learning more and more.

When children feel they need to know something, they are interested in learning it. For example, when parents read to their children often, and when children see their parents reading often, children begin to realize they need to learn to read themselves.

When children grow up, they will need to use math daily. We adults don't stop to think that we are using math when we follow recipes, mark calendars, tell time or check the speedometer.

If we draw children into our own use of math, they'll begin to see reasons for arithmetic. Furthermore, thinking about real life math problems supplies children with practice they need in manipulative and mental-image modes of thinking. This lays a solid foundation for good abstract thinking as teens and adults. With a little thought, we can form the habit of noticing and encouraging children to use arithmetic in all kinds of places:

Math in the kitchen

Encourage children to help you follow recipes. Preschoolers can help count and measure. Older children can learn to follow directions themselves. Begin with recipes for simple snacks like fruit drinks and sandwich fillings. Then move on to more complicated recipes. Bake cookies often!

Young children can pick up a lot of practical math by setting the table regularly. Ask kindergartners to count how many people will be eating a particular meal, and then count out and set the correct number of plates, napkins, and forks. Give elementary age children simple story problems to solve as they work, like "How many places would we need if Grandma and Grandpa were coming for supper, too?"

Math in the grocery store

Let kindergartners count produce. ("Put 8 apples in the plastic bag.") Elementary age children can weigh produce and bulk items, read the numbers on the scale, and compare which is more or less. If you teach children how to count money at home, they can count out the total for small purchases at the store.

Encourage older children to compare prices between name brands or figure out whether or not the cents-off coupon really saves money. Let them add up purchases on a calculator. Or have them estimate the total grocery bill by rounding off numbers and adding them up mentally. Whose estimate comes closest to the actual total?

Math in the car

Read mileage and speed limit signs. Compare the speed limit with your speedometer. Note mileage before and after a trip on the odometer. Count blocks for short distances: "How many blocks from here to the library?"

Math around the house

Count, count, count. Simply counting to 45 is meaningless for children unless they have something to count. So count crayons, buttons, pennies, toys. Teach more advanced number recognition by asking children to look up a certain page in a cookbook, hymnal, or story collection.

Teach children how to use a cell phone to enter important numbers—emergency, Mom & Dad, Grandma & Grandpa, etc. Get a clock with a face and teach children to tell time. Refer children to the calendar. Let them weigh each other. Show them how to take their temperature and read the thermometer. Measure children's height and keep an on-going growth chart. Let kids learn to measure while helping you fix things around the house.

How many hours a day or week are children allowed to watch videos or TV? Figure out which programs to watch within the total family time limit.

Play all kinds of games.

Dominos teaches matching and recognizing groups. Bingo and Uno teach children to recognize and read numbers. When children play board games, they learn to count moves, read numbers, and follow rules. Monopoly teaches a lot of addition and subtraction. Other games teach scoring, logic and strategy. So have fun with your children counting moves, keeping score, discussing strategy, and teaching them to think.

"It is a rather recent phenomenon for us to think that the magic of learning is contained in workbooks," educational author Ruth Beechick said. "But, of course, learning happens in the head. And with young children, real life and real objects can cause more arithmetic to happen in the head than books can."

Further suggestions and instructions for helpful math, reading, and writing aids are found in *The Three Rs*, by Ruth Beechick. Her book is no longer in print, but it's worth ordering from Amazon.com or special order from a local bookstore. ISBN13:978-0-88062-173-1

The Balances of Raising Kids

"Why does the van shake around so much in the wind?" our son Matt asked me one day when he was 7. We got around in two vehicles, a VW van and a small VW truck. "The truck is small and weighs less than the van," Matt reasoned, "so the truck should blow around more. But it doesn't. Why is that?"

Children have questions—many, varied and invigorating to any adult who picks up the challenge of a child's natural curiosity. Children are born with a zest for learning, and it's a sad day when any child stops trying new skills or stops wondering why.

As homeschooling parents, we learned that if we wanted our children to keep their natural delight in learning, we had to provide an environment with balance in these areas:

A balance between safety and freedom

A baby needs to explore—to taste, to touch, to smell, to hear, to see what the world holds. But babies don't survive unlimited exploration without safety features. Toddlers need to run and play, but they also need naps to avoid collapsing from exhaustion.

So parents must provide their growing children with the balance of freedom within safety limits that is appropriate to their ages and stages of development. They must baby-proof their homes, insist on healthy routines, enforce safety rules, model and teach children appropriate ways to vent anger and grief, and provide secure boundaries of discipline with clear guidelines, clear expectations and consistently enforced consequences.

A balance between feedback and pullback

Children need how-to directions for creative efforts like making crafts or writing stories, but too much direction will stifle a child's inventiveness. Our daughter, whom we started homeschooling in fifth grade, hated art in grade school because her teacher insisted that everybody's art project had to look as much like the teacher's as possible to be "right."

Children need adult encouragement and assistance, yet they also need opportunities to work independently and figure things out for themselves. When our Matt first started school at home in first grade, he needed my entire focused attention to help him do his academic work. After his reading and writing skills developed as he turned 10, 11, and 12 though, he needed to learn to work independently.

He was very active, so it was hard for him. If I sat at the kitchen table while he worked, he could stay in his seat for an hour at a time, occasionally asking for help. But if I got bored and started doing housework, he wandered off and disappeared. He couldn't stay on task unless I just sat there—but without hovering.

Crocheting provided the solution. If I sat and crocheted while Matt worked, I could be available to answer questions or provide encouragement when he needed it. At the same time I had useful and satisfying work of my own to prevent impatience. After a while, Matt was able to stick to his work whether I was there or not.

A balance between freedom and responsibility

Children need a good balance between play time and chore time. They gain self esteem and a sense of accomplishment from learning to clean, cook, launder, and do other family chores. In order to develop the ability to have good relationships with others, they must learn to give up some of their own space and privileges to allow others their fair share.

A balance between structured and unstructured time, with appropriate resources.

Children need large doses of unstructured time with good resources in order to discover and pursue their personal interests. But they also need structured time to help them learn ways to use their unstructured time.

When Matt was about 14, he tried to teach himself to play our old guitar. The experience was satisfying at first, but then he got stuck. So we found someone to give him guitar lessons and, with his teacher's advice, we bought him a better guitar.

Matt discovered his interest in the guitar by having unstructured time and an accessible instrument. After he messed around with the guitar enough to decide he wanted to learn to play it well, he needed our help finding more resources – a guitar teacher and a better guitar. After that, our teen spent hours playing his instrument. It became an important creative and emotional outlet, something he did because he loved it. As his skills improved, it also became a social outlet, helping him make friends with other teen and adult musicians – as well as helping to form his spiritual life as he led and played guitar for worship teams.

Homestyle Secrets of the Learning Process

Pneumonia pushed us into homeschooling. Our first grader came down with it twice in six months. I volunteered to help his teacher in the fall, and I soon realized that she would be a poor fit for him even if he was well. Also, the school administration was uncooperative and the office staff seemed unfriendly to children. So I looked into homeschooling and realized it could be a solution for us because the tutoring method would take much less time than the classroom teaching method and our son didn't need the social context of school since he already had numerous outside social outlets.

When I started homeschooling, I had no idea that it would become our family lifestyle. Whenever our two older children got sick and had to be home from school, I included them in our classes. They started begging me to homeschool them, too.

In the end we homeschooled our three children through high school graduation. They all then graduated from the university with honors and went on to graduate school. Our daughter is now a published author, college teacher and publisher. Our first son teaches biology at a community college, and our learning disabled second son is a writer with a Ph.D. in cancer research. All three homeschool their own children, making me a homeschool grandma.

I am convinced, though, that any parent, whether or not they home school, can use the principles we used to make a huge difference in their children's academic progress. Here are the most important ones:

- **The best teacher is the one who loves the child.**

    Young children are natural learners, full of life and curiosity and wonder. As a parent volunteer, I watched our first grader's emotionally detached teacher quench her entire classroom's zest for learning in six weeks flat by publicly humiliating children for minor discipline problems and for not learning quickly enough.

On the other hand, I was touched to see the lengths to which I saw parents without a high school education sometimes go to locate resources for their special-needs children and to educate themselves to learn how to help their youngsters develop to their greatest potential.

Somebody who cares about a child will encourage him over the difficulties, go to the trouble to locate resources he needs, and find out how he learns best. So parents need to connect their children with caring teachers.

- **The quickest, most effective way for children to learn most academic skills is through one-on-one tutoring.**

Most of us get our ideas about teaching and learning academic subjects from our own experiences with the public school system. We don't stop to think that public schools have to be set up for crowd control. Something simple and easy to teach to one child becomes complicated if you have to teach it while managing 20 to 30 wigglers at the same time. At home, for example, you can teach first grade in less than two hours a day, and that includes the time you spend anyway reading to him whether you or a schoolteacher is teaching him.

- **Children are most apt to retain their zest for learning when they follow a few simple safety rules and then are given tremendous freedom to explore within the boundaries defined by those rules.**

This idea is covered in the previous chapter, "The Balances of Raising Kids."

- **Instead of worrying about children's lack of interest in school, begin with whatever fascinates them and move onto other subjects from there.**

Our daughter was burned out on school when she began home school in fifth grade. She had lost her curiosity, and she hated math and science. But she loved to read Laura Ingalls Wilder's "*Little House on the Prairie*" series. So we encouraged her to write her own historical fiction stories, like Wilder.

When she found that project satisfying, we read her a fictionalized science book about a Mississippi mud turtle and encouraged her to model a story on that idea. Soon she was studying science—reading about birds and then writing stories about them. Eventually we gained enough momentum from the motivation she experienced writing in history and science to coax and encourage her past a mental block in math.

(Note: A 4-H program is a great resource for parents looking for ways to encourage a child's special interests.)

- **If you can't tutor yourself, find a resource (book, podcast, video, computer program, home school cooperative, or person) who can.**

Every child needs a good education manager—a facilitator, an encourager, and a resource locator. Although we home schooled our children, we did not teach them every subject ourselves. We used the services of neighbors, graduate students, and friends; we traded teaching duties with other home school parents; we used community resources like classes at the Museum of Art; and we encouraged our older children to teach the younger ones.

We used the library a lot, too. As an eighth grader, our son Erik knew far more than either of us about desert ecology. We just let him roam the desert next to the house and drove him to the library every other week to find books on animal tracking and edible desert plants. Then when we took walks with him through the desert, he taught us.

Preschool at Home

When we were raising our children back in the early 1980s, we had a neighbor, Mary, who was a good mother to her preschoolers. She fed them balanced meals and established a healthy routine of playtime, nap time, mealtime, and bedtime. She kissed their "owies" and dispensed Band Aids with sympathy. She read them stories daily, she limited their TV viewing, she encouraged them to help her dust and cook, and she talked with them throughout the day while she worked, answering their questions and chatting about whatever intrigued them.

Mary taught her children to share their toys with preschool friends who came to visit. She taught her 4-year-old daughter how to cut paper with a pair of blunt scissors and let her 2-year-old son paste, color and paint alongside his sister.

Today Mary would be eligible to send her 4-year-old to Head Start, but back then everyone had to pay for preschool. And although Mary's children seemed to be bright, secure and well behaved, her friends and relatives convinced her she wasn't a good parent because she was not sending them to preschool.

To fend off the social pressure, Mary found a job to pay preschool tuition. She had no education beyond high school, which meant she had to work more hours for less money. Once she began working, she found she had to earn enough money to cover not only preschool fees, but extra expenses of work—wear and tear on the car, more taxes, a wardrobe for work...(It takes $3 earned to equal $1 not spent—so she had to earn $600, for example, to make a $200 tuition payment.)

Sadly, I watched this young family's stress level soar. And for what? Mary was not getting a job to meet personal emotional needs or to make it possible for her family to survive financially.

She was wearing herself out and complicating her family's life to fend off social pressure. Then she paid other people to do something she already did well herself. And liked doing.

That was nearly 40 years ago. Soon afterwards our family joined the homeschooling movement, and I learned about many good home school preschool programs available for parents who, like Mary, lack confidence in their own abilities or prefer a structured plan.

What home schoolers have learned about children and education is available to all parents through a rich variety of educational resources, not only for school age children, but for preschoolers as well. Buying a program is unnecessary, though, as long as these basic elements are present:

- **A warmly responsive, loving parent.**

    If a parent is unavailable, a grandparent or other adult can provide what is needed, as long as the adult is committed to the child long term and is there every day. This person is key to the child's sense of security and intellectual development. Nothing stimulates a child's intellect or builds good social behavior like a warmly responsive, consistently caring adult who talks to her throughout the day, responds to her needs, encourages creative efforts, sets healthy limits, provides calm order and is usually available for conversation.

- **Healthy routines in a healthy environment.**

    Preschoolers need reasonably predictable routines to feel secure. Someone must be sure they eat balanced meals, take naps, do their simple chores, go to bed at a set time, and get plenty of fresh air and several hours of physical exercise daily. If there is no safe yard available to run and play, they need someone to go with them on long walks and play "Tire'Em Out" games. (More on that next chapter.)

- **Materials and encouragement to create.**

    Preschoolers need lots of materials available for spontaneous construction or dramatic projects— a sheet to drape over a table for a tent, boxes, rocks, sand, dress up clothes, scrap lumber. When preschoolers are encouraged to use their own ingenuity to produce their activities, any item in the house can become a toy or a prop.

As much as possible, preschoolers need ready access to toys and creative materials. Toddlers will "read" more if there are a lot of hard-to-destroy children's books around, for example. Preschoolers will draw more if the paper and crayons are kept on a shelf they can reach.

- **Daily reading.**

One school district made a bumper sticker: CHILDREN WHO READ WERE READ TO. The best way to encourage children to become readers one day is to read to them when they are small and keep on reading books aloud as a special shared activity after they begin reading themselves.

- **Rest and solitude.**

According to child development researcher Raymond Moore, 3- and 4-year-olds who do not take a nap or have at least an hour of rest daily become overtired and then are unable to sleep well at night. They can then become chronically irritable and hard to handle.

Children at this age not only need a regular rest time, Moore says, they also need a period of solitude, playing alone with blocks or making roads in the sandbox. "This seems to provide the opportunity he needs to work out certain problems and fantasies," Moore said.

"Genius has been shown to thrive with a great deal of parental warmth combined with ample opportunity for solitude," Moore says.

(See also the chapter "In Praise of Naps.")

- **Positive social modeling and guidance.**

Children learn through observation and imitation. When they are surrounded by a lot of other children (whose social behavior is naturally immature), they imitate them. Preschoolers learn sharing and other social tasks best when they have only one or two other children to relate to at a time, and when the

group is supervised by an adult who is a good model.
- **Involvement in homemaking activities.**

    Preschoolers develop a sense of accomplishment and positive self worth by working alongside a warmly responsive parent in cooking, dusting, sweeping, kitchen cleanup, gardening, sorting laundry, etc.

- **Field trips and nature experiences.**

    When preschoolers plant seeds and watch them grow or discuss what they see and sense on nature hikes and field trips, they collect a lot of essential information about things they will study formally later on. A nature hike can be as simple as a stroll through a garden, and field trips can be as simple as a trip to the store or a walk down the block to look at a road or a house under construction.

- **Freedom from academic pressures.**

    Preschoolers need to collect and make sense out of a lot of information before they are ready to begin formal learning. Too much academic pressure at this stage can result in unnecessary learning problems later.

Tire 'Em Out

Years ago we drove to another city with friends to see a youth musical performance. We arrived at the church early and decided to wait outside in the parking lot because 5-year-old Jacob was feeling restless after being cooped up in the car for 45 minutes. He needed to stretch and be active before having to endure a long bout of sitting still and behaving himself during the performance.

The church yard had just been flooded for irrigation, so a big pool of water stretched along the back edge of the church parking lot. Jacob said he wanted to throw rocks into the pool.

We had no objections, but he needed more activity than that to stretch his muscles from the long ride and tire him out sufficiently to make him want to sit for a while.

So I invented a variation on the all important game for taking long drives with children: Tire 'Em Out. I made up a game rule: You Can't Throw a Rock into the Pool Until You Run to the Fence and Tag It and Run Back for Me to Give You a Rock.

Playing Tire 'Em Out

It was an excellent exercise game. Jacob ran all the way across the parking lot to the fence, tagged it, and then ran all the way back to me (his exercise), while I bent over and picked up a nice fat rock (my exercise).

I also cheered him on and told him what a fast runner he was...and what a big splash he created...and now he was probably too tired—right?—to try it again....

He grinned and puffed and threw rocks and insisted he wasn't too tired and galloped off again to tag the fence until he had managed four or five round trips from the fence to the pool. And then it was time to go into the church, and he was content to sit still for a while.

Children like being active

Why do children cooperate with such adult scheming?

I don't know. All I know is, Jacob was happy, and my children used to be happy, too, with this sort of game—as long as they had my full attention, as long as I cheered them on as they ran, and as long as their muscles truly required a good stretch after a long drive.

Using Tire 'Em Out for school at home

Homeschool parents and families in lockdown can take the Tire 'Em Out principle and use it to turn math, reading, spelling and other subject drills into a game. You can do a math drill lesson at the top of a big flight of stairs. If your student gets the math fact correct, she gets to hop down one step. By adding activity to drills, you make the drills fun for kids. Later when your child really knows her facts and needs more challenge, you can speed up drills by tossing a ball. You call out the problem, count two, toss the ball, and see if she says the answer before she catches the ball.

Tire 'Em Out has endless variations, which you can usually invent on the spot the way I did with Jacob. Your first object for the game is to encourage kids to uncramp their muscles from sitting to do school work or spending a couple hours in the car. The second object is to get kids so tired out that they don't mind sitting down to read a book for school at home or they don't mind getting back in the car to sit a while longer on long trips. The younger or more active the child, the more often you need to spice up schoolwork or take these kind of breaks on long trips.

Using Tire 'Em Out on long car trips

On trips, the playgrounds and parks you pass along the way are especially good places to stop for Tire 'Em Out sessions. But if you think you may become so stuffy brained from traveling that you won't be able to think up interesting ideas for Tire 'em Out, then don't leave home without a Frisbee or a tennis ball in the trunk so you can play catch on breaks. In fact, it's a good idea to develop the habit of packing a ball or Frisbee every time you take a long drive, because as children get older, they usually prefer a game of catch to invented variations of Tire'Em Out.

At home, keep a handy list of ideas for activities to use for drilling or taking active breaks from paperwork and bookwork.

Troubles with Math?

"My son has trouble with division," a woman told me once. "I think it's because he hasn't memorized his multiplication facts."

She explained that her child had figured out his own method for getting the right answers to multiplication problems. He just kept adding the multiplied number mentally until he had added it enough times for a correct answer. His multiplication method was slow, but it gave him right answers. Division had him stumped though. He couldn't figure out the problems.

Although it may not appear that way, this boy's trouble with division was a lot like 6-year-old Jacob's trouble with addition one day when I asked him, "How many places should we set for lunch today?"

Using math in the manipulative mode

First Jacob counted himself and me. Then we talked about the other people who would be eating lunch with us – my husband (who was working in the garage), Grandma (who lived in a mobile home on the back of our lot), and Daniel (who was asleep in the loft).

Jacob couldn't figure out how many places to set. If all five people had been there in the room, he would have easily found the answer. But since he couldn't see the people to count them, he couldn't figure out the addition.

I tried having him put up a finger for each person we named, but he was still confused. He didn't understand that method. A person isn't a finger. How do you count people by counting fingers?

This is a developmental characteristic.

Three math modes

Adults use three ways of thinking about math: the manipulative mode, the mental mode, and the abstract mode. They can switch back and forth, using the abstract mode, for example, to figure using only symbols ($50 - $22.48 = $27.52), or the manipulative mode to do the same problem by counting correct change into a customer's hand.

Young children like Jacob, on the other hand, can think only in the manipulative mode. They have to see and touch objects in order to understand math concepts like adding and subtracting.

Using the mental math mode

As children develop they progress into the mental mode. When Jacob was older, he could do math problems like this mentally – to count me and himself, then mentally image the other three people and count them, too.

Representing each person with one finger, and then counting the fingers, required more mental imaging than Jacob was ready for. We solved the problem by drawing a picture of each person. When Jacob counted the pictures, he knew how many places to set. Pictures of objects help children make the transition from the manipulative to the mental mode of thinking.

This process was a slow way to get my lunch table set, but a good way to teach Jacob basic math. Practicing addition with pictures and objects helps children develop a strong concept of what addition *is*. And until they understand with their eyes and hands what addition is all about, there is no point in having them memorize addition facts.

Meaningless memorization falls out of people's brains. Children have to develop a strong mental image of a particular math process, like addition, before memorizing math facts has enough meaning to make the facts stick in their heads.

Pushing the use of mental and abstract math too soon

The little boy who had trouble with division probably had trouble memorizing multiplication tables because he lacked a strong mental image of what multiplication and division mean. The multiplication tables by themselves were too abstract for him because he had not moved successfully yet through the mental mode of math.

"When we say that a child doesn't understand something (in math), we usually mean that he is not able to image it in his head," said Ruth Beechick in *An Easy Start in Arithmetic*. "The cure for that is to provide more manipulative experience."

Why math manipulatives are essential

Using math manipulatives helps children to develop and strengthen the mental images they need for understanding math concepts. It also helps them to become able to do mental math (which they must learn before being able to do abstract math).

What does 3 x 4 *mean*? It means you have three 4's – that is, three groups with 4 things in each group. What does 12 divided by 3 *mean*? It means you have 12 things in a group, and then you separate those twelve things into three different, equal groups.

To teach multiplication, take a number of counters like pennies or beads and put them on the table with several index cards. Show children how to demonstrate a simple problem like 3 x 4: take 3 cards, place four counters on each card, and count up the total. Three 4's make 12. Children can draw pictures to demonstrate problems, too. For example, 3 x 4 could be drawn as 3 trees with 4 apples on each tree.

When children can demonstrate easily that they understand what multiplication means, then you can show them what division means. To demonstrate 12 divided by 3, count out 12 counters, lay out 3 cards, and put one counter on each card, going round and round until all 12 counters are on cards, and each card has the same number of counters.

So don't rush

"Try showing something one way and a second way and a third way" said Beechick. "Wait awhile and teach it again next month. After sufficient manipulative experience, the child eventually will image the troublesome process in his head. He will understand it."

The chapter "Kids In Touch with Math" includes ideas for using math manipulatives.

Training vs. Setting Kids Up

Once I had a dream that changed my parenting. Our 4-year-old son Erik and I seemed to be battling constantly. *What's wrong with us?* I wondered one night as I drifted off to sleep. *Why can't we get along?*

That night I dreamed that Erik and I were playing a board game. Whenever Erik started to get ahead of me, I became anxious and changed the rules. No matter what, I had to win.

That's all wrong, was my first thought on waking up. *Erik is just a little guy. I should be **helping** him **learn** to play the game, not worrying about winning or losing it.*

"Our" problem was with me

It dawned on me then why Erik and I were having so much trouble: we were engaged in a power struggle stemming from *my* childishness. No matter what, I had to be right (and he had to be wrong), I had to win (and he had to lose).

But being a good parent has nothing to do with competing. A good parent is a good teacher, equipping, enabling, and encouraging children to become the best they can be—physically, mentally, socially, morally, emotionally, spiritually.

It's my job to provide firm limits

Of course children need firm rules. They lack the experience to develop healthy habits, make wise decisions, and understand natural, long term consequences on their own.

A 4-year-old who runs into the street without watching for cars may get away with it a few times, but eventually he'll get hurt—possibly killed. Likewise, a child who punches and kicks other children to get what he wants is developing a pattern that will lead to a life of crummy relationships and the emotional problems that result—unless he learns to change the way he treats people.

It's my child's job to test those limits

But even though children need firm limits and consistent, logical consequences, they balk at them. They resist rules, test boundaries, challenge authority.

So Erik still attempted power plays even after I stopped viewing him as a rival who was challenging my control and started seeing him as an inexperienced little guy who needed firm, compassionate guidance. The power struggles became less frequent, though, and our relationship became friendlier because Erik sensed that I was really on his side.

How can adults avoid the control trap?

My controlling attitude was unconscious and self-defeating. And it undermined Erik's discipline. "Control leads to passive aggressiveness or rebellion," said Izzy Mora, family support coordinator for Parents Anonymous of El Paso.

Adults fall into the control trap, Mora said, "when they believe their way is the only valid way there is—when there's no recognition of the child's personality, opinions, or ability to make decisions." But since the controlling attitude is unconscious, how can parents learn to recognize it in themselves? Mora gives several suggestions:

- **Check your focus.**

    "A controller is only interested in getting a child to behave or perform," Mora said. "He or she is not interested in how the child is feeling or how the child is processing the confrontation."

- **Check your emotional reactions.**

    Whenever controllers feel their authority is threatened, Mora said, they get angry.

- **Check the way you handle your angry and resentful feelings.**

    "Parents need to notice when they're using emotions to control their child," Mora said. "Saying something like 'Get away, I don't want to be near you,' is using emotions to control children into behavior you agree with."

"It isn't good to stuff or deny emotions," Mora said. "If you deny emotions, they fester. Instead you need to give yourself time out—take personal inventory through writing in a journal, through writing a letter that you never send your child, or by asking yourself, 'Why am I so angry?' When you understand why you are angry, Mora said, solutions seem clearer.

"People need to understand that all feelings are OK but all behavior is not OK," Mora said.

- **Check your behavior for a lack of respect for your child.**

When parents yell, nag, or insist on a double standard, for example, then respect is no longer mutual, Mora said.

"Remember that children are little people who are learning life," Mora said. "As adults we are sharing what we know. When children take what we teach, they may do more with it—they may go beyond what we know. We need to realize that instead of only being interested in being right."

Working With — Not Against — Life Seasons

When I was a young mother, my heart's desire was to write. My major in college was journalism. Since my parents were unable to help me much financially, I worked my way through college by winning scholarships and working at a variety of jobs. Now, married with three small children, I thought I should be using that hard-earned education, right? I should be writing for publication.

But.

But I had an undiagnosed thyroid condition, so I needed a lot of sleep. And my children were young. Needy. Matt was an exuberantly curious toddler with a genius for tearing the house apart. (His pediatric dentist nicknamed him Crash.) Erik was a kindergartner who kept begging me to teach him to read. Jessica, age three, stopped taking naps and insisted on being wherever Mommy was.

I kept trying to retire from the circus to write, but the circus kept following me.

One day, just after I'd scolded Jessica for not giving me a minute to myself, the thought dropped into my head, *If you keep telling this little girl every day to go away and leave you alone, when she gets old enough, she'll do it. Permanently.*

At that moment, I realized I didn't like the mom I had become—irritable, impatient, angry. There are laid-back, healthy women who can balance the frustrations of deadlines with preschoolers gracefully, but I was too intense. I couldn't focus on getting published and still have patience for the constant needs of preschool children.

My children's interruptions were keeping me from writing, and my impatience with the interruptions were blocking my mothering. So I wasn't getting published, and I wasn't being a good mother, either.

A time and season for everything

It dawned on me that the author of the book of Ecclesiastes in the Bible was putting his finger directly on my parenting problem when he said, "There is a time for everything, and a season for every activity under heaven" (Eccl 3:1).

When I set my writing goals and made plans to publish, I neglected to consider the season of our family's life. This was not the season to concentrate on getting published. It was the time to teach our kindergartner how to read—while he was eager to tackle the new skill.

Nor was it the season to start the grinding process of assessing markets, sending out queries, and obtaining writing assignments to launch a free-lance writing career. It was the time to build our daughter's self-confidence, by accepting her companionship and encouraging her to work alongside me during her short bouts of enthusiasm for housework.

And, although I made the decision reluctantly and with tears, this certainly was not the time to feel sorry for myself. It was the time to retrieve my sense of humor, recognize Matt's search-and-destroy missions as normal, and let our toddler's exuberance rub off on my soul.

But did all that mean it was the time to stop writing?

NO! Although the season for *publication* was later, there was no need to thwart my writing desire—just to redirect it. Edith Schaeffer's wise counsel in her book *The Hidden Art of Homemaking* encouraged me to be willing to lay aside public ambition and develop my writing gift behind the scenes, in ways that enriched the lives of the people in my house and in my heart.

So I kept a journal. I wrote down the funny things the children said and did. I composed letters to relatives and friends, and I used stories about the children from my journal to make the letters interesting. And then, before I knew it, a half dozen years later I found myself regularly publishing for an audience of 100,000, writing family features and weekly parenting columns for *The El Paso Times*.

Working with the season instead of against it brought rewards

It turned out, unexpectedly, that by working with the season instead of against it, I gained everything in the end that I had hoped to achieve when I tried to focus on publishing instead of parenting. My writing seasoned through my children's preschool season. Describing the children's funny remarks and poignant moments taught me how to write anecdotes. Composing chatty letters to loved ones established a personal writing tone. And throwing myself into the task of parenting gave me a wealth of material to write about when the season for publication finally came.

All the while maintaining and growing healthy and loving relationships with my kids and husband.

And Speaking of Seasons...

In *"401 Ways to Get Your Kids to Work at Home,"* author Bonnie McCullough and Susan Monson list **three learning seasons of childhood:**

- **Spring (age 2 to 5):** When parents need to establish basic routines, lay a foundation of obedience and develop a youngster's confidence.
- **Summer (ages 5 to 12):** When parents need to provide children with training for many jobs and require consistent performance.
- **Fall (ages 13 to 18):** When parents need to encourage teens to take on adult responsibilities.

Taking Walks

Walks are for friends. And walks build friendship in a family. Something about walking sets the mouth in motion. Good news, bad news, plans, dreams, worries—it all starts spilling out as you tramp along.

Walks can build relationships

My mom and I used to take walks when I was a teen. She was a good listener, which made for good talks. As we chatted and listened, we formed strong ties that grew naturally into a healthy adult friendship that sustained us both.

Walks are for scientists, too.

When I was a child, I loved the outdoors and hated science. I made no connection between the two. Nature was alive, wondrous, refreshing. Science was dull. Then I married a geologist. He and our three children showed me the connection.

Walks can teach

Before I met Dennis, I enjoyed beautiful scenery, but I missed a lot. I never noticed the layer patterns in mountains, for example, or wondered how mountains came to be. Dennis tended to explain the scenery, though, and he made me more aware as we walked.

The children made me more aware, too. Sometimes that happened because they were curious. They stopped to inspect ants that I stepped over. They looked underneath bushes that I passed by.

Their delight with the natural world and their ready questions forced me to choose between either destroying their healthy curiosity with indifference or joining them in exploring wonders and searching out answers.

Walks can stimulate

At other times, I became more aware while trying to help them be observant.

One fall day I was walking along an arroyo in the desert with our 7-year-old son when I noticed that we were stepping over many clumps of yellow flowers. "See those flowers," I asked, pointing out the dainty blossoms at our feet.

Then I had a brainstorm. "Now, see all the yellow ones out there?" and I pointed across the desert at many faraway patches of bright color. "Let's try to see how many different kinds of yellow flowers we can find."

So we did. We picked one bloom from each variety we saw, to make comparisons, and then we started counting. I thought we might find three or four varieties. Instead, we discovered more than a dozen different kinds of yellow wildflowers on our mile-long hike. Ever since, I have been tuned in to wildflowers.

Walks can help you slow down

Walks have slowed me down to listen, to talk, to share, to ponder, to observe. The family and I needed it. Good relationships are what healthy marriages and families are all about, and you can't build sound relationships on the run.

"Strong families cannot be created like fast food," columnist Cal Thomas once observed. "They require a commitment of time and loving concern that too many have been unwilling to make."

Walks are for friends, for nature lovers, and for families. But walks are also for me—for my sanity, my perspective, and my renewal.

Walks can quiet your soul

Sometimes my walks with the children used to slow me down so thoroughly, I came to a dead halt. I couldn't watch ants as long as a preschooler could. A hill of soft, fine sand discovered in the desert could keep our 8-year-old son occupied for an hour, but I'd lose interest.

I learned to be glad for those dead-halt times, though. Chunks of quiet were good for evaluating, for counting blessings, for thoughtful prayer, and for simply savoring the goodness of life—for letting myself drink in the beauty around me and soak in the specialness of the child, so absorbed, who pushed me into slowing down to enrich my day with quietness.

Preventing Parent Burnout

I used to be a burnout veteran. I burned out regularly every other year until my pastor pointed out my problem: I was so focused on meeting everybody else's needs, I neglected my own. I was like the little kid who gets so caught up helping his friend build a backyard fort that he wets his pants. So after fifteen years of experience in mothering, I developed Becky's Potty Training Principles for the Prevention of Burnout:

Quit dancing around and go to the toilet.

That means: Learn to recognize and do something about your needs before things start getting out of control.

When my pastor told me to replenish myself by caring for my own needs, I discovered a problem. I didn't know what my needs were. I understood the importance of exercise, rest and proper diet. But my pastor pointed out inner needs that were just as important: needs for solitude, prayer, time with friends, mental stimulation, spiritual growth and creative expression.

Sometimes religiously oriented parents assume it isn't spiritual to have needs. The Judeo-Christian faith, with its practice of weekly rest, is more realistic. The apostle Paul wrote his young friend Timothy to say he was lonely and asked him to come quickly and bring along another young friend, Mark (1 Tim 4:9-13). He also asked Timothy to bring his cloak and parchments. He recognized and admitted physical needs (winter was coming, so he would need his cloak to keep warm), intellectual needs (he wanted his parchments), and emotional needs (he longed for his friends).

Use the bathroom.

Junior is not allowed to use the bushes or the neighbors' front porch. Inner needs likewise must be met in ways that take other folks into consideration. Many people get confused here. Some trample all over other people's welfare in the name of self-fulfillment, while others, wanting to avoid selfishness, go to the opposite extreme and ignore their inner needs altogether.

The solution is to build a bathroom in your house – that is, build a routine solution for meeting personal needs into the fabric of your week. For me, when the kids were all living at home, that included getting up early for some quiet time with God before the family woke, writing a journal, keeping a weekly date with my husband, and trying to get together regularly with close friends.

It's up to you.

Only Junior can tell when his body begins to signal that his bladder is filling, so Junior is the guy responsible for doing something about it. Adults, likewise, are responsible for noticing and dealing with their own personal needs. You are responsible for yourself. However...

Ask for help when you need it.

If the family is shopping when Junior needs to go, he's supposed to tell someone. Likewise, if Mom needs a break, she can ask somebody like Dad or a friend for help.

Sometimes people have to insist. Sometimes Junior's parents don't want to be inconvenienced by a trip to the bathroom en route to the checkout counter. They say, "Can't you wait?" when he can't. His body is sending its signals to him, not to his parents, so he must be the one to judge when it's time to take action.

Taking care of genuine needs cannot be postponed indefinitely. Parents potty-train children to prevent messes. They need to take burnout prevention measures for themselves for the same reason.

Biology and Late Blooming Readers

My homeschooling friend Jane had a little boy named Kenny who was uninterested in reading. When he turned seven, she grew frustrated and started pushing it every day. "He started to stutter," she said, "but I didn't get the message."

I didn't realize what was going on in Jane's home. I just remembered that she had told me once that Kenny wasn't interested in reading. So one day when I was in the neighborhood, I dropped off some material about late-blooming readers.

She said when she read the material I brought, she felt like my visit was like the Voice of God telling her, "Quit Pushing!"

So she quit the daily reading lessons and let her son play with his Legos, which was what he liked to do. "He started making the most amazing, creative, intricate inventions," she said. "He quit stuttering, his self-esteem went up dramatically, and he just blossomed." A year later, she tried reading lessons again, and this time they "took." Kenny learned to read fairly easily.

Many intelligent children, like Kenny, are not ready to read at age 6.

Some of these late bloomers are not merely intelligent, they are geniuses—like Thomas Edison.

Why is this so? If a child is smart, why can't he read?

It's biology.

Each child has his or her own timetable for physical development.

The pituitary gland controls the developmental calendar, says child psychologist James Dobson in his tape, "The Late Blooming Child," and no amount of parental anxiety or social pressure can speed up that timetable.

One aspect of growth that the pituitary controls is myelination. This is a process that insulates a child's nerve pathways with a white, fatty substance that makes electrical impulses move quickly and efficiently to other parts of the body. First each nerve pathway (or axon) must grow to a certain diameter. Then a myelin sheath begins to form gradually around that axon, like the layers of an onion.

Until myelin begins insulating the axons of a particular body system, electrical impulses cannot pass consistently through the nerves in that system. It is then impossible for the child to control that part of his body. His control develops gradually as myelination develops gradually. This is why babies do not all start to sit, stand, or walk at the same age.

The last body system to become fully myelinated (sometimes not until age 8 to 10) is that part of vision that allows reading to occur.

Raymond Moore, former director of the Hewitt Research Foundation, compiled research from neurophysiologists, ophthalmologists, psychologists and research psychiatrists during the 1980's. He said their results consistently show that children learn to read more easily after their vision, touch, hearing, and muscle coordination become more developed, and after they develop the ability to reason abstractly.

When pushed, children can learn to read before they are fully ready, if the axons are partially myelinated. Children can do it, but it frustrates them because they are working without the necessary tools.

Think of trying to flip pancakes with a piece of aluminum foil instead of a spatula, Moore said. You can do it. But you can't do it well. If that was the only way you had to make pancakes, it would be so frustrating, you might decide to quit making pancakes.

Pushing children to read before they are ready is counter-productive.

When children are pushed into reading before they are ready, he warned, they become frustrated and discouraged. Then, by age 8 or 10 when they have the neurological ability to pick up the skill easily and run with it, they are burned out and have lost their motivation for schoolwork.

The solution for late bloomers, Moore said, is to let them wait. Instead of pressuring them to read, respond warmly to them one-to-one. Provide an environment that encourages them to explore, create and think. Read them a wide variety of books, and encourage them to make discoveries and love learning. Work on developing their language and thinking skills.

How we used these principles in our family

My husband and I stumbled across Moore's research reports in 1984, soon after we started home schooling our late blooming first grader. Moore's studies gave us encouragement to back off and allow our late bloomer to follow his own reading readiness timetable at home.

Instead of pushing him to read, we read good books to him. We explored the desert, visited museums, drew maps, created crystal gardens, experimented with art media, and made crafts. And we talked, talked, talked about all the things we did.

Our son developed a wide vocabulary and a strong sense of good grammar and proper English by listening to good literature and engaging in stimulating conversations. This also taught him to think. Then, when reading finally clicked for him at age 10, he caught up fast.

Late bloomers will catch up if they don't get too discouraged by being pushed too early too soon.

Our three children all began reading when they were ready to read. Our early bloomers learned to read at the ages of 5 and 6, and our late bloomer learned at age 10. Yet by age 13, all three were reading at a college level. (And today our late-blooming reader has a Ph.D. in cancer research.)

As a nation we are causing unnecessary damage, stress, and wasted effort by being impatient with children's normal development and pressuring teachers to make all their students learn to read by age 6. As homeschoolers, we were free to refuse to bow to this social pressure and devote our efforts instead to providing the kind of stimulating, literature-rich environment that encouraged our children to love learning and read when they were ready.

The key is providing a language and literature rich environment.

A language-rich environment puts in place the tools children need for using what they read when they become able to read. This environment is good for all children. In our home, we found out that the kind of place where late bloomers can thrive is the sort of place where early bloomers thrive, too.

The Lazy Parent's Secret

Once upon a time there lived a Suzuki mother who was frustrated with her daughter because she resisted practicing her costly, pint-sized violin during scheduled practice sessions. Also, her little girl kept forgetting to put her violin away high on its shelf in the closet down the hall after she practiced. So one day Mom just left the violin out all day in plain sight, hoping her daughter would get the hint and put it away where it belonged.

Surprise! Her daughter never put the violin away. But every time she passed through the room and noticed it, she picked it up and practiced for a few minutes. She wound up practicing an extra half hour more than usual that day.

This is a true story, and it illustrates the The Lazy Parent's Secret for Getting Your Kids to Do What You Want. The secret has two parts:

1) *Remove roadblocks to the behavior you want*
2) *Add roadblocks to the behavior you don't want*

For the Suzuki mom, that meant "If you want your daughter to put her violin away, make it easy – not hard – to put away. But if you want her to use her violin often, keep it someplace handy."

This principle works in many areas of family life (as long as you have a good relationship with your children so that they aren't organizing their life around the goal of upsetting you).

Developing musical and artistic talents

If you teach children how to use musical instruments and art materials properly, they will use them, not abuse them. If you store the tools of music and art where children can get them easily, they will experiment and play around with them to the extent of their interest and ability. If you throw in a few encouraging words ("Honey, I just love to listen to you play that piece!"), they'll do it all the more.

For toddlers, this means you leave the piano lid pushed back and show them how to use one finger on each hand to plink on the keys. It means you leave chalk out for them to draw on the chalk board. For older children it means hanging the family guitar on the wall in the family room where they can take it down easily. It means keeping art supplies in a drawer they can reach, close to a table or work surface they can use any time. It means keeping craft instruction books handy, too.

The way you apply this principle must be modified, of course, to the maturity level of each child. For a toddler, you make it easy to get the chalk but not the markers, because a toddler is too immature to control his impulse to draw on walls. Chalk washes off walls easily, marker doesn't. So put roadblocks in the way to the markers. Keep them up high and allow toddlers to use them only under supervision.

Getting rid of time-wasting distractions is another aspect of removing roadblocks to activities you want to encourage. If children have electronic screens in their room, for example, they will be distracted by them and will text, play games, and watch videos or TV programs instead of exercising their talents and imaginations. So add roadblocks to screen viewing. Keep electronic screens stored somewhere inconvenient when you don't want kids using them. Make it hard to use screens, but easy to use musical instruments and art supplies.

Reading, writing, and learning for pleasure

Keep your coffee table books, illustrated science and art books, etc. in the family room in easy reach instead in a formal living room. Give school-aged children their own books and children's magazine subscriptions as gifts for birthdays and Christmas. Then give them a bookcase for their bedroom. They will be more apt to read for pleasure if the books and magazines are handy. Children will be more apt to write their own letters, stories and poems, too, if they have paper, pencils, and a desk or table to write on in their own room.

Developing good eating habits

If you buy milk and juice instead of soft drinks, your family will drink milk and juice instead of soft drinks. If you put out a plate of carrot and celery sticks for the family to munch on while you fix dinner, they'll eat them because they're hungry and because the vegetable munchies are handy. So buy potato chips and junk munchies infrequently, and when you have them in the house, store them someplace inconvenient. Meantime, keep fruit washed and available in a bowl on the counter. Make it easy to eat healthy food and hard to eat junk.

Putting things away

Most parents are like Dennis and me—we tried to teach our children to be tidy and pick up after themselves before we learned those lessons well ourselves. Fortunately the Lazy Parent's Secret works on lazy parents, as well as their offspring. So I learned to store things close to the place where people use them. That made it easier for me to train myself (and my family) to put them away when we were done. I stored the frying pan close to the stove, kept the basketball in a cabinet by the door nearest to the basketball hoop, and put hooks in the back entry door for the kids to hang up their coats.

There really is no lazy, easy way to be a good parent. Quality parenting takes time and effort. There are ways, though, to spend your time and direct your efforts to bring about more effective results. So if you want children to do something, show them how and then make it as easy as possible. If you don't want them to do something, make it difficult.

Kids in Touch with Math

You don't have to be a math whiz to prepare your preschooler for school math or to help school-age children understand and practice their math. Just keep in mind that children learn math concepts best by beginning with their sense of touch. Here are a few easy ways to introduce or reinforce basic math through touching:

- **Picture Counting**

   Ask your preschooler a "how many?" question when you look at pictures in storybooks and magazines. "How many arms? How many dogs?" At first you will need to take your child's hand to touch or point to each picture, doing the counting yourself. Later, as he catches on, he can point and count by himself. Begin with lower numbers and move gradually to higher numbers.

   If you forget to touch or point to each picture, though, your child may learn to recite numbers without really understanding how to count objects. As your preschooler gets better at this, he will become able to count objects by looking only, without touching.

- **Number Cards**

   To teach number recognition, read counting books that show the number with the items counted on that page. In addition, write the numbers 1 to 10 on index cards. Show your kindergartner or preschooler how to arrange them in order, counting aloud. When she can do this easily (which she may not do until first grade), make cards for numbers 11 to 50 and let her arrange them on the floor in a path.

   Eventually she will be able to arrange cards in a path from 1 to 100, especially if you show her how to sort numbers into piles by 10s before arranging the path, with all the 20s in one pile, all the 30s in another, etc. This simplifies the task and introduces the idea of Base 10.

- **Hallway Number Line**

    Make a big number line along a hallway or up a stairway by rolling out 100 inches of shelf paper, plus a few extra inches for each end of the number line. Mark each inch from 1 to 100 on a line. Then paste a large sticker at every tenth number and a small sticker at every fifth number.

    You might want to place groups of stickers around certain numbers, too—like a group of 3 over number 3 and a group of 20 below number 20. Also, it's a good idea to laminate your number line to keep it from ripping. When the number line is tacked up, children can use it to practice addition and subtraction. The same problems you give kids using the 100 chart can be used with the number line. (See "The 100 Chart" on page 139)

- **Base 10 with 10 Bundles**

    Use rubber bands and a big box of leftover crayons or popsicle sticks from the craft department to help school age kids understand that a big number can be separated into 10s and ones.

    For example, to teach that 23 equals two 10s and three ones, write the number 23 and ask your child to count out 23 popsicle sticks (or crayons or pencils). Then count 10 sticks from the pile, put a rubber band around them, count 10 more sticks and bundle them up with a rubber band, too. There will be three sticks left over. Show your child then that 23 sticks is the same as two bundles of ten and three singles.

    Make up a problem or two every few days until your child thoroughly understands the concept. Later you can use the bundles of 10 to demonstrate regrouping when you add and subtract double-digit numbers.

- **Double Nine Dominoes**

    Nearly all the math concepts a kindergartner or first-grader needs to understand can be taught using double 9 dominoes. Just play dominoes with your child a few times and then add a rule that every time a player puts down a domino, she must state the addition fact shown on it correctly. After a few months, when she is familiar with addition, you can switch to using the dominoes for subtraction. (Count the total dots, then put your finger over the dots on one side and state the problem and the solution.) Give extra chances while your child is first learning the concept. The idea is for her to win at learning math, not for you to beat her at a game of dominoes.

At the end of each domino game, invite your child to join you in setting the dominoes up on end in a line, giving one end of the line a push, and watching them topple. You do this to end each session on a fun note. So if she accidentally bumps the domino line too soon, don't get irritated. Just laugh and start over.

Music Enriches Family Life

I had just deposited our 22-month-old son's breakfast pancake on his high chair tray one morning, when he started singing "Up above the world so high, like a diamond in the sky."

I was astonished. Our baby knew the words to "Twinkle, Twinkle Little Star!"

Our baby can sing!
Matt's vocabulary was exploding, but I had no idea that he could carry a tune. Or that he could repeat a whole phrase from a song.

At the time our two other children were 7 and 4. Like most children their ages, Erik and Jessica were fascinated with musical instruments. Whenever I sat down to play the piano, they stopped whatever they were doing, dashed to the piano bench and begged me to play one of their songs.

So, for a few years, I gave up working on my own pieces and learned arrangements to folk songs and children's songs. I also bought a couple of good song books with pictures on every page so the children could find their favorites themselves. I played and we all sang. They often danced, marched or made up actions to some of the tunes as well. And the baby always included himself in these song sessions.

How many songs does Baby know?
After hearing him sing at breakfast, I started wondering how much Matt had picked up while I was concentrating on his brother and sister's love of music. So I ran an experiment. I sat him next to me on the piano bench, and over several days I played all the songs we'd come to enjoy together. At some point in each song, I quit singing for a line and listened carefully. If Matt carried on without

me, filling in the blanks with the right words, I counted that song as one he knew.

It turned out our baby knew over 50 songs!

Sharing music with kids

Parents don't have to be professional musicians to share the fun of music making with children, to develop a youngster's appetite for good music or to uncover a child's natural talent. In fact, parents don't even have to play an instrument themselves to expose their children to the delights of music. They only have to begin wherever they are themselves and learn along with their children.

Here are some ways to encourage the family's appreciation of good music:

- **Sing.**

   Sing in the shower, and sing as you do chores around the house. Buy albums of children's songs and your own favorite songs, and then sing along, around the house or in the car driving. As children grow older, teach them to sing rounds. This provides a foundation for learning to sing harmony later. Include songs in your children's bedtime routine. Break through whiny, fussy times with singing or listening to music.

- **Introduce your children to music making.**

   Take advantage of children's natural tendency to enjoy blowing whistles and banging drums. Show them how to clap in rhythm first, and then how to keep time using rhythm instruments. Haul out any instruments you play yourself and learn to play the melodies your children like. If they ask for music lessons, take them seriously, especially if they are showing other active signs of interest, like picking out tunes on a keyboard. Even if a child only takes lessons for two or three years, the experience will give him a basic understanding that can provide a foundation for a lifelong appreciation of music.

- **Expose children to a wide variety of music of different forms, styles and cultures.**

To get an idea what different kinds of music the family likes before buying albums, listen to a broad range of music on youtube.

- **Listen actively to music with children.**

    Before you introduce a folk song to a preschooler, for example, familiarize yourself with it first, and then prepare him by telling him a little bit about the song. (Example: "This is a silly song about a goat who ate somebody's shirts. It's called 'Bill Grogan's Goat.' We're going to find out what happened to that silly goat.") Next, listen to the song with him, and then talk about it. This will not only develop his ability to appreciate music, it will also help him develop good listening skills he will need later in school.

Good beginning classical pieces to introduce to children are those that tell a story, like "The Nutcracker Suite," and those that have special sound effects. I was unfamiliar with Saint-Saens' "The Carnival of Animals" until my mom gave me a record of Whittemore and Lowe's performance with the Philharmonic Orchestra. Each of this composition's 14 movements represents a different animal. We played the record, I told the children which animal each movement represented, and we mimicked the beast, miming and dancing around the living room. It was great fun—and great exercise. It became one of the children's favorites, and one of mine, too.

Music enriches all of life. When parents introduce their children to the joys of good music, they are passing along a lifetime treasure.

Nature Hikes and Expeditions

When we moved to Vinton, Texas in 1984, the population included more jack rabbits and horny toads than people. The village consisted then of little more than a few houses on a half dozen streets, a couple small trailer parks, and several wonderful, large tracts of undeveloped desert.

Right away we started taking nature hikes with our children, ages 7, 10 and 12. We skirted cactus tangles, rubbed the seed-wings off the salt bushes, and startled flocks of scurrying Gambel's quail. We hiked up and down dry arroyos, collecting wildflowers and pointing out the places where the last rush of rainwater had collapsed portions of the arroyo banks and exposed the roots of bordering creosote bushes.

Our children also explored the desert with each other on their own, and we let them take our binoculars along, even though the binoculars got banged up. We also bought several cheap magnifying glasses and left them handy for the kids to use whenever they wanted.

After about a year, our oldest son Erik developed a passion for the desert. He borrowed library books on insects, animal tracking and edible desert plants. Following the instructions he read in one of the books, he learned to sit still for half an hour or more until the desert creatures accepted him as part of the landscape and began hopping, calling, slithering, and twittering past.

For our sons, these family nature hikes led to careers in science. Today Erik is a biology professor. His younger brother Matt also pursued science, earning a Ph.D. degree in cancer research before he switched to writing fiction and publishing literary science books. Our daughter pursued a career teaching college English writing and publishing books. The first book she wrote and published was a book on hiking in the El Paso area. All three still love to be outdoors hiking and exploring.

Dennis and I felt that formal science was a weak area in our home schooling, but our children's nature explorations nevertheless gave them a big boost for understanding textbook science later at the university. One good nature hike is worth hours of formal classroom study.

Here are a few ways to encourage children to explore the natural world.

- **Observe and collect plants.**

    Plant your own trees, flowers or vegetables, and get children involved in weeding and watering. Collect wild flowers and interesting plants. Make art projects with children by pressing flowers and then arranging and laminating them with clear contact paper to make greeting cards or bookmarks. Children may also enjoy placing a flower or leaf under a sheet of paper and then rubbing a crayon lengthwise over the plant to see the effect.

- **Look for bugs.**

    Use any glass jar to collect bugs. Just punch air holes in the lid or secure a piece of pantyhose over the mouth of the jar with a rubber band. Dampen a cotton ball for moisture and add a few weeds to make the bug feel at home. Then let it go after you have observed it a while. If you want to make a bug collection, dampen the cotton ball with rubbing alcohol instead of water, and use a jar and lid without air holes. When the bug dies, mount it with a pin. Use a bug guide to help you identify and label your specimens.

- **Look for rocks.**

    Streams and dry creek beds or arroyos are good places to find interesting rocks. Scrub them with water to see them better. Sort and store them in egg cartons, using a guide to identify them.

- **Go stargazing.**

Staying out late and sleeping under the stars is a great family memory maker. If you live in a populated area, the best way to see the stars is to go camping in unpopulated areas where light pollution is less. Take along constellation charts from the Internet or find a good book on astronomy.

However, even if you can only camp out in your back yard where there is light pollution, you can still see some of the stars. You can read your charts or book by flashlight while your children look up at the night sky. A telescope or pair of binoculars is useful, but not a necessity. Your family might also enjoy having you read about the mythological creatures the constellations are named after, like Hercules and Perseus.

- **Watch birds.**

  Attract birds with a bird bath or a bird feeder near a window where the family can watch. Use binoculars to see birds best, and be sure to bring binoculars along on hikes.

- **Buy hands-on science materials.**

  Keep magnets, magnifying glasses, bug jars, gears, electrical sets, and other science materials handy for children's play.

- **Add variety to your hikes by checking out special places to see.** Visit local parks, nature centers, and museums. Phone ahead to see if you can time your visit to take advantage of seasonal educational programs.

Hooray for Mother Goose!

Mother Goose was one of the few books I packed along during our family's great adventure in Kenya in 1973. At the time, our oldest son Erik was nearly 2 years old. My husband was spending six months on a scientific expedition in northwest Kenya, collecting data for his Ph.D. research. Erik and I joined Dennis during the last three months of the expedition.

I packed only what I could physically carry while still managing to hang onto a toddler through the airports of Chicago, New York, London, and Nairobi. I brought only clothes for me and Erik, a couple of toys, and a few essential books.

Mother Goose entertained

Mother Goose entertained us on planes, in hotels, in tents, and around campfires as we began our nomadic adventure. The first month nearly every day was different—we drove through forests, mountains, and wildlife preserves; we lumbered along beach roads and lurched into the canyons and over the trackless plains of the desert in our four-wheel drive truck. We stayed a few days here, a few days there.

During the second month we lived in a tent in the North Kenyan desert next to a dry riverbed. We followed that up by camping the third month at another desert location near bleak cascades of high rock.

Mother Goose provided security

But no matter what changes we experienced, *Mother Goose* lent stability to our toddler's day. Every day, Jack and Jill went up the hill to fetch a pail of water. Little Jack Horner never failed to sit in a corner. And you could always count on the spider to sit down beside her and frighten Miss Muffet away.

Our African neighbors found *Mother Goose* appealing, too.

The Turkana of northwest Kenya were a people straight out of the pages of *National Geographic*. The women wore skirts made of goat skin, and they encased their necks in dozens of bead necklaces made from ostrich eggshells. The men sported mud pack hairdos and went naked except for a single length of cloth, which they usually wore slung under the left shoulder and tied at the right shoulder.

Mother Goose enchanted our neighbors

One afternoon I was reading *Mother Goose* aloud to Erik under a thorn tree. A young Turkana tribesman wandered by and started peeking over my shoulder at the pictures. I let the young man take *Mother Goose* over to the dining table, where he was soon joined by a bare breasted teenage girl and two young male warriors carrying long spears.

It was a comical sight—four half-naked Turkana seriously contemplating the pictures in *Mother Goose*, puzzling over the cat with his fiddle, solemnly discussing the cow jumping over the moon....how I wished I could understand the Turkana language for just five minutes!

That copy of *Mother Goose* is no longer with us. When it started falling to shreds, I bought another copy for our second child. And then I bought a third copy for child number three. We seemed to wear out one *Mother Goose* per child.

Mother Goose helps lay an English language foundation

A bilingual kindergarten teacher told me that she always teaches *Mother Goose* rhymes to her children because it helps them learn English. *Mother Goose* ushers children into understanding and appreciating the English language. It is a foundation for later reading and writing.

The rhymes are easy to learn and fun to repeat. Repeating them helps reinforce the meaning of the words. The absurd images stimulate a child's imagination. The color and the cadence of the words introduce children to the sheer delight of language. The illustrations and the rhymes together pull children into an enjoyment of the world of books.

Twenty-five years ago, 5-year-old Jacob started coming to our house every day during the summer while his mother worked. When he first came, he had little interest in books and little patience for reading. But soon he was sitting still for 20 or 30 minutes while we read to him.

For him, I bought our fourth copy of *Mother Goose*. And today, with 13 grandchildren, I've kept on buying, and I've stopped counting.

Educate with an "I Love You"

It was one of those awful moments, my mom once confessed, when she realized she had let her child down.

She couldn't remember anymore what my brother had done to deserve the scolding she gave him before he left for school. What she always remembered afterward, though, was the dejected curve of his little back as he trudged up the sidewalk to begin another day at school.

"Defeated and discouraged," said the slumping back and trudging gait.

Well, maybe he bounced back. Children do. Still, Mom said, she realized that day that the way she said good-bye to her children in the morning set the tone for their day at school. So after that she made a point to send them off with a hug and a kiss and an "I love you."

A child's education is primarily the responsibility of his or her parents. Schools exist to help parents with the job. Children do best in school when parents and school staff work together as partners.

Here are some ways to be a good partner:
- **Encourage your children.**

    Listen and talk to your children, really paying attention to their words and feelings. Show an interest in their schoolwork and hobbies. Praise their work and display it.
- **Train children to develop good work habits.**

    Limit screen time, teach children to do regular chores, and set a regular routine for schoolwork, meals and bedtime.
- **Spend time with your children in activities that stimulate the mind.**

    Read stories daily even to youngsters who can read themselves. (You will be building your child's vocabulary and comprehension by reading material beyond her reading level.) Play board games and card games together. Help with hobbies, visit the library and explore local parks and museums.

- **Know what's going on in your children's school.**

  Look through textbooks, visit open houses and parent-teacher meetings, introduce yourself to your children's teachers. Volunteer if possible. Try to get a feel for the atmosphere your children learn in daily. Are teachers encouraging and loving, but firm? Or do they rely on put downs, constant threats and public humiliation to keep children under control? Do teachers encourage or discourage questions?

  Encourage teachers who try hard and do well, and do your part to develop a partnership relationship with teachers and administration. But remember, partnership is a two-way street. When an administration considers parents to be an unwelcome nuisance, their attitude is a caution signal.

- **Be open to alternative educational solutions.**

  A school that works well for one child might not work well for another, or a school might work out well one year and be disastrous the next. So parents might look into transferring their child to a private or parochial school. On the other hand, maybe all they need to do is ask the present school to change a child's teacher or educational program.

  Home schooling is another alternative. A growing number of parents are successfully teaching their children at home through all the grade levels, while other parents find that just one or two years of the personal attention and one-to-one instruction that home schooling can offer, may turn a defeated child's attitude around or get him over an academic or social hump.

Training Kids to do Housework

The teen years have a reputation for being the worst years for raising children, but I disagree. A well-trained teen can be so marvelously competent.

Take the time my gall bladder nearly blew up and landed me in emergency surgery. Our three children were 17, 14 and 12. For several months, with a little help from Dad, they completely took over all the cooking, housecleaning and laundry. The two older ones also planned and completed all their schoolwork independently (we were home schooling).

When parents take the trouble to teach children good work habits, skills and attitudes when they are young, it really pays off when they get older. Here is an effective training method for teaching school age children the basics of those housecleaning chores they will need to handle all their lives:

- **Decide which tasks your child can reasonably be expected to master over the next couple months, and work out a reward system for learning to do them.**

    This system should include a major, long term reward, such as a special outing or purchase, as well as smaller, intermediate rewards, such as points or payment for work accomplished. These smaller rewards help children see their progress, encouraging them to keep trying.

    Most children need both a carrot and a stick. The reward is the carrot. The stick is a consequence that is uncomfortable enough that the child will prefer to avoid it. A simple consequence might be: you must stay in this room until you have completed your work; you may not play outside or in the house until the job has been approved.

- **On a card write down each step in the correct order needed** to accomplish the job.

Example: "The bathroom is done when
1) the mirror is cleaned
2) the vanity is straightened and wiped clean
3) the sink is scrubbed..." (etc.)

(Remember always to list "Cleaning supplies are put away" as the last step. Otherwise children will leave supplies out.)

- **For easy reference, place the direction card permanently in the area to be cleaned.** For example, the living room card can be taped inside the coat closet, and the bathroom card can be taped inside the medicine cabinet.
- **Demonstrate each step and then ask your child to do the work while you watch.**

  Be sure to show your child how to use the direction card as a checklist, too. This is essential for consistent results. And don't forget the reward. Depending on the age and ability of your child, you may need to work together in this way several times before allowing a solo performance.
- **When he appears ready, ask him to do the job alone.**

  When he says he is finished, inspect his work with him. Read the direction card aloud, checking if he did each listed task. Chances are, he will have neglected to use the card as a checklist and tried to rely on his memory. If so, stand around patiently while he finishes the steps he skipped, and be sure to praise him for each task he does right. When he achieves the independent work stage, increase his reward or give an extra reward.
- **Be patient with this process.**

  Children don't see dirt without training or learn to use a checklist without practice. You will frustrate yourself and discourage your child if you expect adult behavior or immediate professional results from a beginner.

Training children to do chores involves three parenting principles that are the same for effectively training children in every area of life:

- **First, clear expectations.** (In this training method, the direction cards provide clear expectations children can refer back to each time they attempt the task.)
- **Second, definite consequences:** the carrot and the stick.
- **Third, consistent follow up.**

Be sure to check the job and follow through, making sure the reward is given or the negative consequence happens.

When training is haphazard, with chores expected one week and ignored the next, children balk. They accept chores more willingly when parents communicate their expectations clearly, give plenty of praise, discipline rebellion, and behave as if chores are a given of life.

You want your child to think, "The sun rises every morning in the east, and I clean the bathroom every Saturday."

In Praise of Naps

When our daughter Jessica was three, nap time became such a hassle that I gave up and let her play. After all, I reasoned, Jessica had never needed as much sleep as her older brother had at the same age. I assumed she had stopped needing a daily nap.

I made no connection between our daughter's lack of rest during the day and her inability to sleep well at night. I was too tired to think things through clearly partly because of health problems and partly because my own sleep was so interrupted—I was frequently up at night with our new baby or with Jessica.

**No daytime nap,
poor nighttime sleep,
poor daytime behavior**

At night Jessica slept restlessly and suffered from bad dreams. During the day, she was often irritable and hard to manage—all symptoms, I realize now, of her lack of a regular, daily nap.

"There is both research and clinical evidence," said education specialists Raymond and Dorothy Moore in their book *Home Grown Kids*, "that children (ages 3 to 5) who do not either nap or have at least an hour of very quiet rest time during the day are not able to get to sleep as well at night. Because they are over tired, they...are restless and more susceptible to bad dreams."

"This poor quality of night time sleep makes them vulnerable to fatigue again the next day," they went on. "A vicious cycle is established, and then parents wonder why the children are excitable, irritable, hyperactive, and difficult to handle."

"My kids need naps!"

Claudia Milhalov, mother of three children, ages 6, 4, and 11 months, decided that her children needed a rest time no matter how much they protested. "Kids bounce off the walls the tireder they get," she said. "I noticed that a lot of times Paul (age 4) would protest and then fall dead asleep. There was no relationship between how much he protested and whether or not he needed sleep."

Claudia insists on a rest time because "we all need the break. I deserve a down time even if it's only an hour." Claudia's son Paul usually sleeps during the family's rest hour, but 6-year-old Carrie rarely sleeps. "If she's cranky or if she went to bed late the night before, I say 'Please try to sleep today,'" Claudia said. "But otherwise she can read or do something quiet."

"The advantages are now coming out," Claudia said. "Carrie is using her quiet hour with a lot more initiative than I imagined. The other day after rest time she said, 'Look at the story I wrote!' She thought up that idea herself."

Carrie recently told her mother, "I've decided I like my quiet time because I know then for an hour I'm going to have time that Paul won't bother me."

Here are a few suggestions for reducing children's resistance to nap time:

- **Be consistent.**

    Children balk less if parents act like nap time is one of the givens of life, like daylight and nighttime darkness. "You have to have the discipline to arrange your day so you are home at 2 p.m. (or whatever time you choose for a regular quiet hour—you can adjust it)," Claudia said. "Kids resist naps more when the structure of their days is haphazard."

- **Provide routine consequences for missed rest times.**

    "(Our children) soon discovered that getting to stay up longer or even go someplace in the early evening was adequate reward for the regular nap," the Moores said. "One or two consistent experiences of being deprived of this privilege—the routine consequence of no nap—helped them understand the cause-and-effect relationship. Physical punishment or

scolding in such cases is neither productive nor necessary."
- **If necessary, help children wind down with a relaxing nap time routine.**

    When I was regularly babysitting our young friend Jacob, age 5, I helped him relax by reading him a few stories. He slept better if I remained in the room, so I spread a sleeping pad on the floor for him and then lay down on the bed myself. I set the timer for 30 minutes, and I told him, "You don't have to go to sleep as long as you keep your eyes closed and don't peek until the timer dings."

    Invariably he fell asleep—and I usually did, too, if I didn't peek for half an hour either.

    Other helpful methods that the Moores suggest: give a back rub; turn on quiet music; "cuddle like spoons" or let the child cuddle up with a stuffed animal each time; tell a sleepy time animal story in a soft, slow voice.

- **Require one hour of quiet time if children do not sleep.**

    Set a timer, and provide children with two or three choices for quiet time activities—puzzles, workbooks, coloring books, drawing and writing materials, etc.

- **Wake children up gently if they tend to sleep so long in the afternoon that they don't go to sleep at night.**

    Children who tend to oversleep may feel grouchy when you wake them up, so don't upset them needlessly by wakening them abruptly. Play a little music or rub their backs as you talk softly and coax them back to the waking world.

Organize Your Child's Bedroom

How would you like to be told that you have to clean up WalMart all by yourself? In one hour?

Taking into account a youngster's size and maturity level, says *Totally Organized* author Bonnie McCullough, that's the same kind of overwhelming task that parents require when they expect a youngster to keep control of a bedroom that contains all his or her toys, books, clothes, a bed with a fancy bedspread, a set of sheets, a couple blankets, and a brother or sister plus all their things, too.

Children need adult guidance to keep their bedrooms in order, McCullough explains, and organizing a child's bedroom is the first step in helping them even *be able* to keep it neat.

Here are a few of McCullough's tips for organizing a child's bedroom:

- **Set aside a half hour to analyze the room and its problem areas.**

    Sit on the floor of your child's bedroom with a pad and pencil, look at it from your child's point of view and jot down ideas for making it more manageable.

- **Look for ways to cut down on the quantity of items your child must keep in order.**

    Can some items be stored elsewhere? If all your child's clothes are stuffed in his dresser or hanging inside the closet, it might help to remove out of season clothes and clothes he has not grown into yet and store them in cardboard boxes on a closet shelf. Sports equipment might be better kept in a box or closet near the back door.

    Ask yourself if your child really needs all this stuff. If you store some of it out of sight for a while, he may realize he doesn't really use it and be willing to sell it at a garage sale or donate it to a good cause. If a child has too many toys, you can try rotating them—set some aside for a month, and then trade those for ones in the room next month.

The younger children are, the fewer items they will be capable of managing.

- **Look for ways to arrange the room to make it simpler for your child to tidy up.**

   Is the bed easy to make for a child his size? A washable quilt pulled over a fitted sheet is easier for young children to manage than sheets, blankets, and a fancy bedspread. Is it hard for your child to hang up the clothes in his closet? Consider lowering the clothes rod and/or installing hooks.

   Are you expecting Junior to carry his dirty clothes down the hall to the bathroom hamper every night when he undresses? Dirty clothes are more likely to be placed in something handier, like a large plastic wastebasket (without a lid) placed in a corner.

- **Figure out a definite place for everything left in the room.**

   Where do shoes go? Under the bed? Inside the closet? Is there a wastebasket for trash? Is there a shelf for books? Children who have a place for books in their bedroom are more likely to learn to read for pleasure. Where will your child keep school books and homework projects?

   Is there a special place for games and puzzles so the pieces don't get jumbled and mixed together? What about toys? Plastic dishpans placed on shelves make better containers for toys than a toy box, where everything tends to get dumped together into a major mess.

After a child's room is well organized, he will still need patient guidance and assistance to learn how to keep it under control. Parents often need to work alongside children until they are 6 or 7 years old because it takes a lot of maturity for them to keep at the job of picking up or cleaning on their own.

Teens are another story. "During their teens, children go

through a stage when they rebel about keeping up the bedroom," McCullough says. "At this time the relationship is more important than the bedroom, and you need to back off the room issue and rebuild the relationship. If they have kept their rooms fairly neat during previous years, chances are they will return to neatness."

For more tips on organizing children's bedrooms and helping them learn to take care of their bedrooms, read Bonnie McCullough's book *Totally Organized* (St. Martin's Press).

Push "Easy" Books for Reading Fluency

Our son Erik was a visual learner who picked up the skill of reading quickly as a kindergartner after only two or three weeks of simple home phonics lessons. Once he "clicked" on reading, he read all the easy reading books he could lay his hands on. He usually read them through several times.

I thought he was ready for something harder the summer after first grade. By then he read easy books fluently, and he had a hardy attention span. He could sit attentively for a half hour or more at a time while we read him long children's classics at bedtime like C.S. Lewis's *The Lion, the Witch, and the Wardrobe.* So I suggested he try reading *The Wizard of Oz* by L. Frank Baum, a book he was familiar with because I had read it aloud to him.

He was ecstatic to find out he could read a novel length book. Every day he reported his progress: "Mom, I'm on page 67!" or "Mom, I've read 200 pages!!"

**Two bright brothers,
one an early bloomer,
the other a late bloomer**

Not every child is ready to tackle such hard books at age 7. Two children, both equally bright, may reach reading readiness at different ages—even five or six years apart. Our son Matt was a late bloomer who finally "clicked" on reading at age 10. Yet he, too, was reading novel length books within two years after he really began reading.

For both boys the key to moving on to the hard books was twofold. First, as parents we built up our children's vocabulary by reading them many stories that were written well beyond their reading level. Second, as novice readers the boys developed fluency in reading by reading many easy books over and over.

Encourage reading fluency

Author and educator Ruth Beechick states that encouraging reading fluency is an important step that parents (and schools) tend to skip by pushing children on to harder and harder reading materials. This is a mistake, she says, because reading lots of easy books helps developing young readers in several essential ways. First, it gives them practice with decoding skills until these skills become over-learned and automatic. It also helps them learn and relearn the common words that make up a large percentage of all books, including difficult ones.

It helps children read more smoothly and rapidly. It also helps them develop comprehension, instead of losing the sense of a passage while struggling to deal with difficult vocabulary and decoding at the same time. Finally, reading lots of easy books helps youngsters find out that reading can be fun. But what is an easy book? The answer varies from reader to reader.

Each child has three reading levels

Beechick explains that every child has three reading levels at all times: a frustration level, a learning level and a comfort level. (These levels provide a way to rate books, not a way to rate individual children.)

- **The frustration level**

    To rate a book, she says, mark off a section of about 100 words and ask your child to read it to you aloud. If he or she has trouble reading more than five words, the book is at that child's frustration level. It has so many new words that the child cannot follow the sense of the story. Avoid pushing children to read at their frustration level. Set aside the book for a while. Children who are pressured to read books at their frustration level become reluctant readers. It makes them want to give up on reading.

- **The learning level**

    If your children miss three to five words in the 100-word section, the book is at their learning level. This is a book for you to read together, taking turns reading every other paragraph or every other page. Whenever Junior bumps into a problem with a word, you can help him solve it.

- **The comfort level**

    If your children miss two words or less in the 100-word section, the book is at their comfort level. It's an easy book. They can read it independently and understand the story well. It's a good book for a child to read alone or to a younger brother or sister. Reading a lot of books at this comfort level will noticeably improve a child's reading fluency.

    You can teach children how to use a form of this test themselves when choosing library books. Tell them to read a page in the book (assuming that a page will have from 100 to 200 words on it) and use their fingers to count the words they don't know. Whenever they run out of fingers on one hand, the book is probably too hard.

    If parents using this test find out that the simplest books in the library are on their child's frustration level, it means the child does not really know how to read yet. In that case, parents need to back up and teach their child to read using a good phonics program—that is, if the child has reached reading readiness.

Ruth Beechick's book, *The Three R's*, includes information about ways to tell when a child is ready to read. It is no longer in print so it has to be special ordered. It includes a reading section (telling how and when to begin phonics and how to develop comprehension skills) a language section (showing how to develop written language skills naturally) and an arithmetic section (explaining how to teach children to understand math concepts). Beechick explains the reading process simply. She gives directions for providing reading readiness activities, introducing phonics, teaching children to read using real books, testing children's reading level, and tutoring spelling. Order the book from Amazon.com, Christianbook.com or special order from a local bookstore. ISBN13:978-0-88062-173-1

Modifying Games for Children

My dad could be fiercely competitive when he played games with other adults. But when he played with children, the challenge for him changed from winning to figuring out the best way to teach the game.

Dad was a genius at modifying games to help us learn how to play well at each of his children's level of development and ability. We used to have back yard touch football games that included everybody in the neighborhood who wanted to play, from my teen-age brother and his friends to my 3-year-old brother Lee.

Normally teens would be expected to refuse to play touch football with a baby on their side, but Dad changed their attitude. He invented a new rule: Any time Lee's team managed to get the ball into his hands, Lee got an automatic touchdown.

That rule transformed Lee from a team nuisance to a team asset, and it motivated his team to encourage him. As his skills improved, Dad kept on adjusting the rules to keep the game a challenge for him and fun for everyone else, too.

Games provide a wealth of opportunity for children to develop essential learning skills.

For example, Uno, Old Maid, and other card games teach preschoolers matching. Monopoly provides incentive and practice for school age children to figure out basic math problems. Authors and Clue help children learn to reason and deduct. Outdoor sports like softball and soccer help children develop motor skills and hand-eye coordination.

Parents and older siblings can encourage younger children to play games well with a few simple strategies:

- **Introduce rules and strategies with practice games.**
  With older children, play a game or two with the cards face up, explaining as you play. Play with the cards face up all the time with preschoolers.
- **Avoid intense competition.**
  For young children, competition can be "too fierce and emotionally distressing to be enjoyable," said Lincoln Stein, author of *Family Games*. "If you shout, 'Hooray! We've used up all the cards,' instead of, 'Tough luck, you lose,' 3-year-olds will be delighted," he said. "Keeping early play relatively pointless will avoid both the bitter repercussions of letting children win on purpose and the violent feelings that emerge when a family plays too competitively."
- **Simplify.**
  Choose the simplest games for preschoolers, Stein suggested, and doctor the deck of cards, leaving only the Aces, 2's, 3's, 4's and 5's. "Add cards when children are able to recognize names and numbers, to hold more cards in their hands, or their increased skill calls for more complicated games."
  Stein also suggested that instead of shuffling the cards, children can lay them all on the floor face down and pick them back up in random order. If children can't hold all the cards in their hands, he said, use fewer cards. Or place a pillow in front of a child and lean the cards against it. Another solution is to let children hold the cards as a deck and look through it card by card.
- **Invent handicap rules.**
  Modify the game the way my dad did with our neighborhood touch football games.
- **Turn a competitive game into a cooperative game.**
  Let younger children play with parents or older siblings as cooperative partners. A preschooler can sit on someone's lap during a game of Uno, for example, and help choose which cards to play.
  When families play games flexibly this way, they can accommodate not only the younger children, but also other family

members with special needs. My father-in-law developed Alzheimer's Disease. As he became more confused and disoriented, he could no longer play complex games like Scrabble or Monopoly with his grandchildren. But for a long time, he could still play Uno. And he needed to be included.

In our family, it was OK for one of the kids to look at Grandpa's hand and gently tell him which card to play next if he got confused. That way we made it possible for Grandpa to stay in the game as long as possible—the game of Uno, and the game of life.

Attention Deficit Disorder

Michael is 6. He is a special needs adopted child, born with fetal alcohol syndrome. Overly active and easily distracted, it seems like Michael is always in trouble.

"He has to be watched constantly," his mother said. "I know it isn't good, but our family centers around Michael. We have to know where he is and what he is doing all the time."

"He gets in trouble at school because he cannot control his impulses," she said. "He's over exuberant, and he hugs the other kids in kindergarten too much. Since he's responsible for so much that goes wrong, he gets blamed even for things he didn't do."

"Once another child threw a Lego carton," she went on. "The teacher asked, 'Who did that?' and one of the girls immediately said, 'Mikey.' Michael wasn't even in the group!"

Michael has Attention Deficit Disorder (ADD). His 12-year-old sister Charlene has it, too, but her symptoms are different.

"Charlene can control her impulses," her mother said, "but she has trouble processing instructions so you can't tell her more than one thing to do at a time."

"She's very disorganized, too," her mother said. "The other night she was doing her math problems. She could do them in columns or in rows. So she did one column, and then she moved up to the middle of the page—not the top, the middle—and started to do rows. She did the first row left to right and then the next row right to left."

Charlene has been hurt by children who make fun of her for having so much trouble with reading and math. "It's frustrating for the child. It's frustrating for the whole family," this mother said. "Sometimes you forget why this child is having problems."

ADD is caused by a chemical imbalance in the brain

Researchers believe that 3 to 5% of American children are affected by ADD, which is caused by a chemical imbalance or deficiency in the brain. This chemical problem interferes with the way a person is able to sustain attention and focus attention on a task and with his ability to control his impulses. Sometimes ADD is accompanied by other learning disabilities. Symptoms, severity, and treatment vary from individual to individual.

A child is likely to have ADD if he or she persistently and frequently displays at least eight of the following 14 characteristics for at least a six month period before age seven: fidgets or squirms excessively, has difficulty remaining seated, is easily distracted, has difficulty waiting his turn in games or group situations, blurts out answers, has difficulty following instructions, has difficulty sustaining attention, shifts from one uncompleted task to another, has difficulty playing quietly, talks excessively, interrupts or intrudes on others, does not seem to listen, often loses things necessary for tasks, or frequently engages in dangerous actions.

Children with ADD and their parents get very discouraged

Parents of ADD children often see themselves as failures. Their parenting task is draining, and there seems to be little or no reward for their efforts. What works for other parents—and what works with other children in their family—doesn't work with the ADD child. Other people criticize their parenting and disapprove of their child. It hurts. It can take a big toll in the form of shame, anger, guilt, and depression.

ADD children often see themselves as failures, too. People misunderstand them, and they lack the affirmation from others that children need to keep trying in the social realm. Unless these children are identified and given the help they need while they are still young, their educational problems may cause them to fail or drop out of school. Their difficulties in personal relationships may cause them to become seriously depressed, to abuse drugs, or to rebel and get into trouble with the law.

Gayle Seerden, coordinator of the El Paso ADD Support Group, gives this advice to parents who suspect their child has ADD:

- **Get a good diagnosis.**

    "Talk to your family physician about it," Seerden said, "because you need his recommendation for a specialist, like a developmental pediatrician or a psychologist. He will do a lengthy evaluation and ask for a lot of history on your child." He may also recommend medication to improve the symptoms of ADD.

- **Notify your school that you are seeking an evaluation.**

    "Whoever does the diagnosis will want to have evaluation from the teacher," Seerden said. "If you already know your child has ADD, though, go directly to the school for help."

- **Know your legal rights.**

    Public schools must give children with ADD special education and/or related services when necessary. ADD children are guaranteed a free and appropriate public education by two federal laws—the Individuals with Disabilities Education Act (IDEA) and Section 504 of the Rehabilitation Act of 1973.

- **Get information and emotional support through an ADD Support Group.**

    "During the meeting you hear sighs of relief, you see tears," Seerden said. "It's just very comforting to know that someone else has gone through or is going through some of the same problems that you are."

- **Learn how to be your child's advocate and work with the school to help your child.**

    "You are your child's best advocate," Seerden said. "It takes the parents, child, school and medical professionals to keep a balance of normalcy. It takes a lot of adjusting and readjusting to find what is normal for an ADD child."

Note: Homeschool parents of children with ADD can contact NATTHAN (National Challenged Homeschoolers Associated

Network), a Christian non-profit organization that provides encouragement and support to homeschooling families raising children with special needs.

Learning in the Doctor's Waiting Room

Before I started home schooling our children, I used to let a lot of good educational experiences slip right past them. For example, our 11-year-old son Matt, and I spent 6 hours one day at the El Paso MedPlus West and the El Paso Orthopedic Surgery Group waiting around for examinations, X-rays and a cast for Matt's right hand.

Waiting around is irksome, and at one time I would have used those six hours to practice being irked. But once I took responsibility for my own children's education, I developed a different perspective.

MedPlus West actually was an intriguing place if you looked around. There were wall posters showing the skeleton and muscle systems as well as interesting equipment that you don't see around the house every day. So Matt and I inspected the charts to locate the bone that hurt.

Which bone did I crack?

If Matt had had a classroom assignment to memorize the bones in the human body, he would have learned the information only long enough to regurgitate it onto a test. But after he cracked a metacarpal, he became interested enough to look up the term himself. He remembered it and became more interested in the other bone names, too, eventually going on to study biochemistry in graduate school for a Ph.D in cancer research.

After Matt and I inspected the wall charts, Judy Rauch, the MedPlus X-ray technician, took Matt to the X-ray room. I could have waited behind but I tagged along because Matt and I were learning about cracked metacarpals together.

How are X-rays developed?

Rauch was a pleasant, motherly woman who not only answered

our questions about how X-rays are developed but also allowed Matt to go with her into the dark room to watch the developing process. I noticed the lead aprons hanging on a stand and asked if Matt could try one on. Then we talked about why pregnant women wear lead aprons during X-ray sessions. (The lead helps protect the unborn child from excess radiation.)

After that Rauch began volunteering interesting information that we otherwise would have missed. For example, she showed us a pin she wears which monitors the X-ray levels she is exposed to each month. She also showed Matt how heavy the lab doors are. Like the aprons, the doors and walls of the X-ray room are lined with lead. She was glad to discuss in some detail the importance of all these precautions.

Not every worker is like Rauch, of course. Our cast technician was friendly, but not terribly informative. People are different. And we didn't spend our whole six hours of waiting asking questions and looking around. Matt spent some of that time reading his English and history assignments.

Recognizing and taking advantage of life's (sometimes painful) opportunities

The point is that we were able to get some good use out of one of life's misfortunes. The value of time spent this way far exceeded the value of the same amount of time spent in a formal classroom memorizing scientific vocabulary. One hour of satisfying a child's curiosity about the natural world is worth many hours of formal classroom teaching.

Informal, hands-on learning experiences make a child's mind like Velcro. When he encounters related materials later in a classroom, the new information no longer will bounce off his brain. It will stick.

Making the Most out of Bedtime

"If you give your boys a kiss and hug every night at bedtime," a mother of young adults told me when our sons were preschoolers, "you'll be surprised at how long they will still be willing to give you hugs when they get older."

I followed that mom's advice. I kissed and hugged our boys good night at bedtime through their grade school years and beyond. And even as teens, they never became too embarrassed to hug me – even in front of their friends.

I have bedtime to thank for other gifts besides our boys' willingness to express affection – gifts like shared family faith and good family communication.

Many young parents worry about these three areas. They wonder how to pass along to their children their values and their faith in God. They say, "I couldn't talk to my parents. How do I change that for my kids? How do I raise them so we can really talk about important things?" Or they say, "I didn't feel loved as a child. My parents didn't express affection. How can I do better with my children?"

In each of these three areas, a parent's best bet is to take advantage of bedtime.

Communication

Have you ever noticed how talkative kids get when you're trying to put them to bed? Well, don't fight it. Take advantage of it. Set bedtime early enough to include 15 or 20 minutes for this time when children often feel reflective and gabby.

When a child is settled in bed, ask "What was the best thing that happened today?" Bedtime provides an opportunity for children to process the events of their day.

If there has been tension or trouble between you, bedtime

provides an opportunity to try to resolve it. Then bad feelings don't fester unhealed in your relationship. Let children complain, but insist that they do it respectfully. Try to understand how they feel instead of just reacting. Listen actively.

Be willing to apologize if you see that you were wrong or that you misunderstood. Children need a model. They need to know how to apologize and how to right a wrong. You can turn your mistakes into opportunities to give them that model.

When children are troubled, they need to know that there is a time in the day that they can count on to talk privately with you. Bedtime can provide that.

When I was 13, I had a traumatic encounter with an exhibitionist. I didn't have the vocabulary to explain in a few words what had happened, and I was too embarrassed to tell my parents about it when my brothers were around. I knew I would eventually have a chance to talk about it in private though because even though I put myself to bed at age 13, Mom always came into my bedroom to say good-night and chat.

She came, I talked, and she called the police.

Family Faith

Bedtime is a natural time to pass on a family heritage of faith. Even when children get too old for reading Bible story books, parents can still take a few minutes to end the day with prayer.

And if parents encourage children to talk about important matters of the day at bedtime, then it will be natural to talk about faith issues, too. Sharing, not preaching, is the way to draw children near to God.

Convincing Children of Love

What says "love" to a child? A parent's touch, words of approval, direct eye contact, and his or her focused attention are powerful love conductors.

Every child has a love tank. And all children sleep better at night (and do better during the day) if that love tank is topped off. Parents fill that tank at bedtime by looking directly into their children's eyes, giving undivided attention to their children's words, and saying good night with a warm hug and a kiss and an "I love you."

Parents who didn't feel loved as children themselves can practice doing these things with their children every night at bedtime until it feels so natural, they start doing it during the day, too.

Taking unhurried time at bedtime to express affection and let children talk is an investment that pays rich dividends in communication, mutual affection, and shared values.

None of these benefits will come into being, though, unless a parent takes the trouble to make the bedtime routine part of the family's daily schedule. If a parent treats bedtime as one of the givens of life, children will accept it far more easily than if it comes and goes at different times – or worse, if it is open to nightly negotiation.

It helps for parents to realize that one last, important way that parents convince children they love them is by setting and keeping firm, consistent limits. So bedtime can produce some of a parent's and child's closest moments – and some of their earliest battles.

And I'll write about that next.

Bedtime Battles

A family's regular bedtime routine can produce a parent's and child's closest moments – and their earliest battles.

"Having a regular bedtime is part of the parameters that kids need to find security in their home," author and psychologist Kevin Leman said in a recent interview. "Children need to know there's an end to the day and a beginning of the day."

Preschoolers, in particular, need a bedtime ritual.

A typical healthy ritual for a preschooler, Leman said, includes a trip to the bathroom (for brushing teeth, going to the potty, and getting a drink), a story time, a prayer, a tucking in, and a chat "to defuse the day."

"Do not hurry while you are tucking your child in," Leman emphasized. "This is your daily opportunity to communicate your love to your child at a critical moment." Your child is more important than a movie or a TV program, he added.

Talk at the end of the day is still important for older kids

As children grow older, the bedtime ritual grows less important, but taking a few minutes to discuss the day's events is still a good idea. Substantial conversations about feelings, moral values and God are more apt to happen at day's end when children are feeling reflective.

But bedtime produces battles as well as intimate moments. "Kids have wills, and they're going to exert those wills," Leman said. "To be a good parent you must be in healthy authority over your child. Let children know there are parameters in your home, that they don't get everything they want."

"Children need to know that if they get out of bed, they'll incur your wrath," Leman said. "They need to know that you still love them but that there are times you need to really get after them because you love them."

These are a few of Leman's suggestions for winning bedtime battles:

- **Deal practically with night fears.** Use night lights, leave the hall light on, and—very important—monitor television, Leman said. "Most fears resulting in nightmares, night terrors and abnormal thoughts and feelings are a direct result of allowing children to watch violence on television."

  Talk about fears, too, he suggested. "Tell how you recognized and handled certain fears in your own life...Help your child understand that everyone has fears and that with help and encouragement, he can overcome what is making him afraid."

- **End your bedtime routine with an audio book or music.**

  Set a timer and start a story or music just before you leave the bedroom.

- **Give children different bedtimes.**

  "No two children should go to bed at the same time unless they're twins," Leman said. Give an older child the privilege of a later bedtime, he said, even if it's only 15 minutes later. Sending all the children to bed at the same time seems convenient to parents, but "having everyone treated alike breeds contempt and competition among children," Leman said.

  "Kids really are different," he said, "and if you're going to find their natural bent and encourage them, you must treat them differently."

- **Check your expectations.**

  "Realize that kids are kids," Leman said. "They're going to get the giggles sometimes. Choose your battles wisely. It's not terrible if they take half an hour getting to sleep."

- **Provide consequences.**

  Set up a few family rules to deal with the usual stalling tactics. Examples: You get one story, one prayer, one tucking in; if you get out of bed for any reason, you have to tuck yourself back in. No one will bring you a drink after you are in bed. When you don't go to bed on time, you go to bed half an hour earlier the next night—or give up your favorite TV program for a week.

"Children are masters at needlessly involving Mom and Dad in their lives," Leman explained. "They want to monopolize their parents and will go to great lengths to do so. We need to make bedtime the child's responsibility—not ours. If he wants you to bring him a drink, say, 'There's the bathroom.'"

- **Don't arbitrate bedtime quarrels.**

"If two kids are wrangling, don't play Judge Wapner," Leman advised. "Hold them both accountable because fighting is an act of cooperation. Each one has to know exactly what to say to escalate the battle further."

Use action instead of words, he said. For example, give children Time Out in a boring place like the bathroom with nothing to amuse themselves. "Children usually fight for attention," he said. "Take away the audience and the fight usually stops."

Teach Your Child to Read

"Please, Mom, teach me to read," our son Erik begged me one day during his kindergarten year. His request overwhelmed me. I had no training in teaching reading. Besides, with three children under age 6 to care for, I lived in a whirlwind of interruptions with no time to find, choose, and figure out how to use a reading program.

"I don't know how to teach reading," I said.

Erik's eyes brimmed with tears. He *really* wanted to read! "Tommy's mom puts words on the refrigerator," he said.

Well, I figured I could do *that* at least. We had a beginning reader with about 25 simple words in it. I started posting the words from the book on the refrigerator one by one, showing Erik how to blend the sounds of the letters to decode the words. Erik picked up the blending skill right away, so it only took me a minute or so to teach a new word. After a week or so, when Erik knew half the words from the book, we sat down to read it. Soon Erik was reading independently.

Ruth Beechick's "Instant Reading" method

By accident, Erik and I had stumbled onto the rudiments of the "instant reading" method that I later found described in Ruth Beechick's manual *A Home Start in Reading*.

About half of the children you teach will learn to read with almost any method you use, Beechick said in an interview published in 1996. "With the other half, maybe some of them need to wait until they're seven instead of six, or maybe some of them need some kind of a problem addressed first."

"The more problems that a child has," she explained, "the more important it is that you strip away anything that's extra and get right down to what is actually necessary." So here is a stripped down explanation of Beechick's stripped down reading method:

- **Put out trial balloons to see if your child is ready for reading instruction.**

    When children begin asking questions about words and letters or learn favorite books by heart, that's a clue to teach them to write or pronounce one or more letter sounds. "Is he interested in learning them? Or does he resist?" Beechick asked. "Your observations of the child and your trial balloons will tell you when to start. And the same skills will tell you all along the path just how fast to move."

- **Teach the forms and sounds of a few letters.**

    You can bypass learning the alphabet and learning the letter names, Beechick said, and move instead directly to the skill needed in sounding out words. "This makes it an exciting mental challenge—a matter of understanding and not just a matter of memorizing a lot of phonics facts that Jenny is not ready to use yet."

    Learning the alphabet and letter names can come later, Beechick said, although it doesn't hurt if children have picked it up already by watching TV. Beechick's manual suggests a number of games and activities for teaching an active child the sounds of a couple vowels and a few consonants.

- **Teach your child how sounds blend together to make words.**

    For example, if your child knows the short sound of *a* (as in *dad*), as well as the sounds for *n*, *p*, and *t*, you can begin the blending lesson by printing the letters on a chalkboard or paper with the vowel above the consonants, like this:

    a

    n p t

    Point to the a and say the sound. Then teach your child to say it whenever you point to it. Do the same with n, p, and t. Then slide your pointer from a to n and say the word *an*. Have your child say the word whenever you point to those two sounds. Teach *at* the same way. Then move on to three letter words like pan, tan, and nap.

"Blending skill is one of those things you cannot hurry in children," Beechick said. "That really takes a certain mental level." So if a child is not picking up the blending skills, Beechick suggests parents back off and not bother with teaching all the sounds yet. "Wait until he can blend with a few sounds, and then go on and teach the rest," adding new letters to the chart with the vowels on the top line.

- **Teach the rest of the letters and their sounds as well as letter combinations such as th and ch.**
  Waiting to teach all the sounds of the letters until this point is an efficient, stimulating method of teaching, Beechick said, because instead of learning a dull, memorized list, a child can immediately put each new sound she learns into use. "Thus she learns more easily and quickly than she would have before," Beechick said.

The Three R's by Ruth Beechick helps you teach your child reading, math and language skills. The book is out of print, so order it from Amazon.com, Christianbook.com or special order from a local bookstore. ISBN13:978-0-88062-173-1.

Dyslexia Resource: Long after I published this article, I found another excellent resource in *Phonemic Awareness in Young Children* by Marilyn Jager Adams, Barbara R. Foorman, *et. al.*, which our son discovered when he had his dyslexic daughter tested for learning disabilities. Dyslexic children have much greater challenges with reading than other children do. And there are other kids as well who have a harder time than most in distinguishing the differences in the sounds that make up words. While the games in *Phonemic Awareness in Young Children* are especially designed to help dyslexic kids, they are actually helpful for all (hearing) children.

Money Lessons by Age

I don't remember what our daughter Jessica did wrong or even how old she was. I think she was about 6. All I remember was my shock at the way my attempt to provide a simple, logical consequence produced a shrieking melodrama.

Jessica's allowance was a quarter a week, so I thought a reasonable penalty for misbehavior was a three cent fine. It wouldn't bankrupt her, just make her think twice next time, right?

Wrong. When I told my little daughter she had to give me three of her pennies, she reacted like I'd told her I was going to chop off three of her fingers. She wailed, she sobbed, she set the house vibrating with her grief.

It was genuine distress, not calculated manipulation—although I figured if I handled her wrong, she'd learn to put on a show like this again when she wanted her way. I also realized I'd misjudged Jessica's maturity. She was bright. She could count money and make change. But she was emotionally unready to understand its meaning or value.

So I told her we could make change. If she gave me ONE nickel, I'd give her TWO cents. Her tears subsided, we traded money, and I postponed using fines for discipline until she was 9 or 10.

Teaching children to manage money well is a major goal of good parenting. But to do it, parents must understand *what* to teach *when*. Here are a few suggestions from Consumer Credit Counseling Service at the El Paso YWCA for tailoring your teaching to children's levels of emotional readiness and ability to reason:

- **Preschoolers** are concrete thinkers. They have trouble grasping abstract ideas like money, space and time. Since a nickel is bigger than a dime, preschoolers think it's worth more. Checks and credit cards confuse them.

Preschoolers need simple experience buying items at the store. Let them hand the money for purchases to the store clerk at first, and later give them a small amount to spend. Show them items they can buy with that amount. This helps train them to limit spending to a budgeted amount. Above all, don't reward begging by giving in to it.

- **Elementary age children** - First and second graders still find it hard to understand that decisions made today bring on consequences tomorrow. They have trouble making choices and are unable to be realistic yet about what money can buy. Parents can help them by explaining the why of some family shopping choices. Third and fourth graders benefit from doing simple price comparison problems with a pocket calculator and from receiving an allowance.

  In some towns, children this age also can begin running errands, first with an older brother or sister and then by themselves. They can take money in a change purse, and then buy one or two grocery items and bring back the change. These activities are an important step toward being able to shop independently in a few years.

- **Tweens** usually like to shop and are ready to buy some of their own clothes. Since tweens can handle greater responsibility, they can start earning money by doing odd jobs at home and elsewhere—which is fortunate, because their activities with friends, hobbies and school activities cost more.

- **Teens** feel a lot of social pressure to keep up with the crowd—to dress like their friends, do what their friends do, and have whatever "everybody else" has. They want to be independent and make their own decisions, but their financial dependence gets in their way.

  Responsible independence is the goal, and teens can work on that with parents. If they show responsibility handling their allowance, it is helpful to increase the amount to include a clothing budget. Teens are more likely to be reasonable about money issues if they have developed experience handling money responsibly since they were small, and if they understand the relationship between their spending and the family's income.

Next: money management basics through a regular allowance.

Money Management Basics for Kids

From the time I was about 3 years old, my parents gave me an allowance of one penny per year of age. But then one day in fourth grade, when I was 9 years old, my father made the astounding announcement that he was going to increase my allowance from 9 to 40 cents!

My responsibilities would increase along with my cash flow, Dad explained. From that day on I would have to buy my own paper and other school supplies and also save to buy birthday and Christmas presents for the rest of the family.

I could hardly breathe, the news was so unexpected, the possibilities so intoxicating. I felt grown up, in charge, loaded with money and responsibility.

Suddenly new problems demanded solutions: Which store sold paper cheaper? (I learned to scout for bargains, to do comparison shopping, to check the Sunday paper for ads.) What should I say to the freeloader at school who borrowed paper and pencils but never returned them? Now that I would have to take the loss myself, I learned some of the practical reasons for ethics.

My parents showed me how to use my allowance to develop a plan for spending and saving, but as I grew older my wants grew greater than my parents' ability to increase my allowance. So I developed a baby-sitting clientele and used the money I earned to buy fashionable clothes, go to camp, and so on. I learned to sew and make crafts to stretch my gift money and increase my wardrobe for less money.

When a child's income is dependent on what adults can be convinced to provide, the child tends to learn how to manage people instead of learning how to manage money. A regular allowance, on the other hand, can be a parent's best tool for preparing children to manage large sums of money one day on their own.

The Consumer Credit Counseling Service at the El Paso YWCA gives these suggestions for teaching money management through a regular allowance:

- **Wait until your child is ready.** Children under 8 or 9 may not have the patience to save money or the emotional readiness to make the kinds of decisions required for a simple saving and spending plan.
- **Figure out basic expenses.** Help your child keep track of the money he spends for two or three weeks and use that information to estimate how much he needs.
- **Begin with a simple plan.** An envelope system often works well at first. Show your child how to divide his allowance up into envelopes labeled for different purposes—savings, contributions for church or synagogue, lunch money, bus fare, fun money, etc. Decide together on a safe place to keep the envelopes and explain how important it is to take money from the envelopes only when it is needed.
- **Be consistent.** Children need a regular amount paid on the same day each week—or each month for older children—to learn how to plan ahead. Learning to manage with irregular amounts at irregular times is too complicated for children. So if the family income is irregular, parents need to set aside the amount of allowance that will be needed for several weeks and give it on schedule.
- **Make adjustments as necessary.** When children ask for an increase in allowance, they should be able to make an accounting of the way they are spending their money, but not to the penny because it's reasonable for about 10 percent to be unaccounted for. Then they can determine with parents whether the increase is for needs or wants. Re-evaluate regularly as your child's expenses and ability to handle responsibility increases. A teenager's allowance, for example, may be increased to include a clothing budget.

Learning to manage money well is an absolutely necessary survival skill. No child should leave home without it.

Best Toys Are Simple Ones

The other day while driving through a nearby Texas village, I noticed several children digging in a vacant lot. The soil in that neighborhood is so sandy that any vacant lot is just a giant sandbox with creosote bushes growing in it. The kids were obviously having a wonderful time. All they needed besides the sand to stay busy and happy all day, I think, was a bucket of water and a few old containers to make molds and cook sand stew.

The best toys and play materials stand up to hard use and keep a child interested even when his interests change. They are open ended, which means that they can be used again and again in a variety of ways. A molded plastic castle, for example, is less open ended than a set of blocks because, unlike the blocks, the castle always stays the same shape. Blocks not only can be used to form a castle, but can also change into a skyscraper, a zoo, or a road system.

Here are a few simple, open ended toys and play materials that have kept children happily occupied for generations:

- **A sandbox can be plain or fancy.** A well-constructed box with seats is nice, but a plastic swimming pool works, too.
- **A set of big blocks is a must.** These can be expensive, though. You can make your own for less by sawing a couple of two-by-fours into 4, 8, and 12 inch lengths, then sanding them well.
- **Sturdy cars, trucks, and trains that run on kid power** with personalized sound effects are more open ended than the battery driven kind.
- **Dolls.** Buy dress up dolls for school age children and huggable dolls for any age.
- **Flannel board and flannel graph figures.** Half a yard of flannel or felt tacked to the wall or a board or draped over a sofa back gives kids a fine flannel background. Shapes cut from

different colored pieces of felt will adhere to the flannel board. More complicated, individualized figures can be made with interfacing from a fabric store. Draw a figure on plain paper, place the interfacing over it, trace the outline, and cut it out. Color it with paints or markers.

- **Building sets** such as Legos, Brio-Mec, Tinkertoys and Lincoln Logs are worth budgeting for.
- **Stuffed animals** make great playmates and childhood comforters. Avoid products that don't wash easily or that have small parts that a child might detach and swallow or poke into an ear or nose.
- **Puppets** range in price from reasonable to ridiculous. You can make your own from scraps. Google "easy homemade puppets" online for lots of ideas and directions.
- **Modeling clay or play dough** can be kept on hand and used over and over. To make play dough at home, mix 1 cup water, 1 cup flour, ½ cup salt, 2 tablespoons cream of tartar, 2 tablespoons baby oil, and a few drops of food coloring in a saucepan. Stir on medium heat until the dough leaves the sides of the pan. Knead on a floured board and keep in a sealed Ziplock bag when not in use. (For more sculpting recipes, see *Glorious Glop: save money and delight your kids with homemade art supplies, untidy science experiments, and other messy fun activities* in the Bookstore at www.beckypowers.com)
- **Art materials:** crayons, markers, scissors, glue sticks, glue, paste, colored sidewalk chalk, watercolors, colored pencils (older children will enjoy fine, soft-leaded pencils like Berol Prismacolor), poster paint, paste, construction paper, drawing paper, tracing paper...the possibilities are endless. Coloring books with pre-drawn pictures are fine for a wait at the doctor's office, but children need the open ended materials for projects at home.
- **Blackboard and chalk or white board and dry erase markers** are important for kids because their small motor muscles are still developing. Writing big helps them. Buy a blackboard or

make your own. I bought blackboard paint from a paint store and painted a door in our children's rooms to give them giant blackboards. You can buy white board and dry erase markers in an office supply department. Or you can buy white board in 4 x 8 foot panels in a hardware store, and then cut and frame it to the size you prefer.

- **Plastic figures of animals and people** can provide hours of imaginative play time. Choose figures that reflect the values you want your children to hold.

Using the 100 Chart for Math

1	2	3	4	5	6	7	8	9	10
11	12	13	14	15	16	17	18	19	20
21	22	23	24	25	26	27	28	29	30
31	32	33	34	35	36	37	38	39	40
41	42	43	44	45	46	47	48	49	50
51	52	53	54	55	56	57	58	59	60
61	62	63	64	65	66	67	68	69	70
71	72	73	74	75	76	77	78	79	80
81	82	83	84	85	86	87	88	89	90
91	92	93	94	95	96	97	98	99	100

The Hundred Chart is a simple tool that parents can use to help their children learn math. There are as many ways to use it as there are numbers on the chart.

The diagram above shows what a Hundred Chart looks like. You can find many variations online by googling "printable 100 chart." You can also make your own enlarged chart on poster board to hang up in the kitchen or wherever your children do their homework, post a letter-size copy on the refrigerator, and give kids their own copies for different math activities.

Here are a few ways to use your chart:
- **Easy Math**

    After children can accurately count concrete objects like blocks and stones, use the chart to count, first to 10, then 20, and eventually to 100.

    Use it to help children recognize numbers. Which is 5? Which is 55?

    Make an extra-large size copy, cut apart the number sections, and ask your child to make a train on the floor, arranging the numbers in correct order. Start with the numbers 1 to 10, then try 1 to 20. Work up eventually to 100, encouraging your child to wind his number line around furniture or down hallways to make it fit. (You can do the same activity by making numbers by hand on index cards.)

    Show your child how to sort these number cards by ones, 20's, etc. This is an activity all by itself. It also can be used to help children make the number train to 100 without becoming overwhelmed. If they sort the cards, it's easier to make the train.

    What is one more than 7? What is 5 plus 2 more? Count forward to work out simple addition problems on the chart. (You can also do this and many other Hundred Chart activities on a homemade number line as described in "Kids in Touch with Math.")

    What is one less than 8? What is 5 minus 3? Count backward to work out simple subtraction problems.

    Take turns with your children doing problems. Give them the easy ones they are ready for, like 3 plus 4. Let them give you hard problems, if they want, like 59 plus 6. Show them how you figure out the hard problems.

- **Advanced math**

    Use white-out to make three or four number squares blank in

each row. Photocopy the resulting chart and tell your child to fill in the blanks.

Use the chart to count by 10's, then by 5's, then by 2's.

Tell your child to count and color the chart by 3's. Then post the chart where children can see it from the dining table, and tell everyone to count by 3's in unison before they can start eating. Do 3's one week, 4's the next week, and so on. Counting number groups helps children learn their multiplication tables.

Count by 10's, but start on the 4 or the 7. Try starting on other numbers.

Count by any size number you can. Start with any number you want.

Count backwards from 100 by 10's. Count backwards by 5's or 2's.

Add 8 to 5. Add 8 to 15, then to 25, then to 35. This makes a bridge from one row of 10 to another. Try other bridging addition problems.

9 is an interesting number to add because its position is one less than 10. Add 9 to different numbers and try to figure out a rule for adding 9. Then do the same things with 11.

Subtract 5 from 62, then from 52, 42, 32, 22, and 12. Try other subtraction problems with bridging.

- Use the hundred chart to figure out hard problems and homework problems, too.

Treasure Hunts

Family treasure hunts are a fun way to give kids practice and incentive for reading and writing. They're also good if someone needs to be cheered up or if a day is getting too dull, because it's so much fun to follow a trail of clues through the house for a treasure hunt.

The idea is to make a treasure hunt at your child's reading level. (Pictures are a preschooler's reading level.) After they've experienced the joy of the hunt, you can then encourage them to make treasure hunts for you or for each other at their writing level. (Pictures are also most preschoolers' writing level.)

- **Introduce the idea with pictures to preschoolers.**

    The easiest way is by using a digital camera. Take and print out pictures of familiar furniture—the rocker, the refrigerator. If you don't have a camera, you'll need to make simple drawings of the furniture. (You don't have to be a great artist to do this. If your children can't figure out what you have drawn, tell them what it is. Hang onto your sketch to use over again, and next time, they will remember.)

    Show your little ones how to follow the picture clues from the crib in the baby's room to the rocking chair in the living room, then on to the sofa, and so on, following the clues until at long last they come upon—ta da!—new underwear. Or two cookies apiece. (Simple things turn into something special when you find them at the end of a treasure hunt.)

- **If your children are beginning readers, add simple instructions to the pictures**, like "LOOK UNDER THE (picture of the couch)." Pretty soon, your children will want to make their own treasure hunts. Keep a stack of photos or drawings available for preschoolers to arrange a trail of picture clues for other family members. Encourage early readers to add more and more writing to their clues. Even children who "hate" writing won't notice they are getting practice when they're making clue cards for a treasure hunt.

- **As children get more proficient in writing, they may like the challenge of making riddle clues or clues in rhyme.**

    My 9-year-old grandson makes clues for me like "You find it where you eat." Then I look at my place at the kitchen table, and there's my next clue.

    When children ask how to spell words, tell them simply. (No exasperated tones, no comments like "You should know that!") Keep it a fun activity. I didn't correct my children's spelling mistakes on clue cards, figuring that it would dampen their enthusiasm. And besides, it might make my writing-hater quit one of the few writing activities he liked. In time he started correcting spelling himself because he wanted people to be able to read his clues.

- **A fun prize for experienced treasure hunters is dinner.**

    (Tip: it's best to conduct treasure hunt meals outdoors to reduce damage from spills.) At the end of the first two or three clues, the family finds plates, silverware, a beverage, and another clue. A couple clues later, they discover the salad, and everyone sits down to eat it. The family keeps on following clues and sitting down to eat as they find the rest of the meal, including the final treasure—dessert.

Turn Kids on to the Past

Grandparents are children's best tour guides for a visit to a history museum, according to Barbara Ardus, curator of the El Paso Museum of History in El Paso, Texas. The next best tour guides, she said, are parents, aunts and uncles. Relatives make the best tour guides because they can relate museum exhibits to a child's own family history.

"People don't actually have to know history," Ardus said, "if they just treat the visit as an exploratory expedition, asking questions, pointing out things that especially interest them, and relating what they see to their own family history. For example, if they see an embroidered shawl that reminds them of the one Aunt Suzie brought home from the Philippines, they can point it out and tell the children about the shawl and Aunt Suzie."

Ardus said that her own career in history first began when her parents took her and a cousin to history museums near her home in Washington D.C. These family trips did much more to spark her interest in history, she recalled, than school tours to the same museums.

School tours are helpful for controlling large groups of children, Ardus said, but informal, family tours show children how history affects them personally. Also, children learn more with one to one attention. Ardus suggested several ways for parents to encourage children to discover and enjoy history:

Find children's histories, biographies and historical novels in the library and read them with your children.

Then when you visit the museum you can relate materials like suits of armor and scrub boards mentioned in the books to similar things they see in exhibits.

Look into the history of your own hobbies and special interests.

Every subject from space travel to embroidery has a history. Once you know something about it, you can relate that information to materials you and your children see in the museum.

Instead of reading museum labels to your children, share the information in your own words, relating bits of history to things your children already know.

For example, you could compare the heavy wooden wheels on a Spanish ox cart to the rubber wheels on your car or your child's bicycle.

Ask each other who, what, where, when, why and how questions.

Whose was it? Where did it come from? How was it used?

Bring your unanswered questions to museum workers.

Some museums will research a subject for interested visitors who leave their name and phone number.

Subscribe to magazines like *American Heritage* and *National Geographic*.

Youngsters may not read the articles, but the pictures will spark their curiosity. Children can pick up a lot of historical information just by reading these magazines' picture captions.

Toddlers Helping

Our son Matt was the kind of toddler who was into everything. I used to feel like I spent my days just following him around and putting the house back together. One morning when I went to our bedroom to make the bed, I found that 18-month-old Matt had discovered the basket of clean laundry and strewed clean clothes all over the room.

I picked them up, made the bed, started down the hall and noticed that I had left the linen closet door open. Matt had removed and scattered the contents on every shelf he could reach. I picked it all up and proceeded to the living room, where I found that he had removed all the books from the low bookshelves and scattered them everywhere.

Harnessing energy

Matt wasn't being deliberately naughty. He was active and curious, that was all. And I needed to learn how to harness that energy, for his sake and mine. My first mistake was picking up all that laundry myself. What I should have done was to go fetch Matt and show him how to help me put the laundry back in the basket, then sort and fold it—not as punishment, just as a simple chore that he and I could enjoy doing together.

Inviting children to work alongside you

Including young children in your work helps keep them busy and occupied in a constructive way—directing their energy to help instead of hinder and building within them a strong sense of self confidence, belonging, and personal significance.

"The earlier you start including them in family chores," my friend Rosie Jones says, "the more the concept of helping and being of service in the family sets into their hearts." Rosie should know. She raised eight children.

What can toddlers and preschoolers do?

"What kind of work can a toddler or preschooler help with?" I asked Rosie years ago, when she still had little ones at home. Her words are still spot on today. Here's what she said in 1994:

- **Pick up chores**

    "Even our little Joshua, who is 11 months old, helps pick up," Rosie said. "He started walking at 8 months. As soon as they start to walk, you can start teaching them to pick up their blocks, books, dolls, and cars. You make it a game at first. You count 'One, Two' as you pick up."

- **Laundry Chores**

    Folding and sorting laundry is another chore. Andrea, age 2, likes to help her mom and her older brothers and sisters with that job. "At first, toddlers just sort out the underwear and socks," Rosie explained, "then gradually they learn to fold."

    "They start by folding washcloths and small hand towels," Rosie said. "They learn to match up the corners, and that builds up their motor skills. Then they learn to fold diapers and carry the stacks of diapers to the bedroom. It's a big help for everyone."

- **Housework**

    Toddlers and preschoolers can save a lot of wear and tear on Mom's knees by dusting base boards and lower parts of the furniture, Rosie said. "We have a lot of antique furniture, and Andrea loves crawling around with Timothy (age 5) dusting below knee level."

    "And the toddlers love to take the throw rugs out and shake them," she said. "It makes them feel big because they can shake all that dirt out of the rugs."

    "Preschoolers can help by stripping the beds—from about age 4," Rosie said. "They help with the pillowcases, too. One holds the case and the other one stuffs the pillow into the case."

- **Sweeping and mopping**

    Some preschoolers can learn to sweep and mop. "Our Gabriel could hold a full-sized broom when he was about 3," Rosie said. "He loved to sweep, and he would sweep the corners and the edges. To this day he's like that—very consistent and neat with the work he does."

    "Mopping is another fun thing," she said. "If you want to be that daring, let a 4-year-old do it. Two of the boys mopped the whole kitchen for me one morning while I was changing the baby's diaper."

    "First they watch you sweep or mop, back and forth, row by row," she explained. "As a mother, you need to speak out your procedure—make a little chant or song to a rhythm—and they learn with that. Then you let them do just a little, not so much."

- **Kitchen Chores**

    Young children enjoy helping cook. "They like to get up on the kitchen chairs and help by stirring and mixing," Rosie said. "I get it started, and then all the brothers and sisters take turns. Then when it's done, everyone gets a lick of the batter from a spoon. So there's a reward."

    Toddlers like to help parents or older siblings set the table, Rosie said. The older ones count out the forks and let the toddler place one at each plate. Toddlers and preschoolers help with many of the small steps involved in setting the table, like taking plastic mustard and ketchup containers from the refrigerator and setting them out on the table.

    Preschoolers can learn to clear their own place after a meal as well. "When they're about 3 years old we have them start taking their silverware and plate to the sink to soak," Rosie said. "They shouldn't carry it all at once. They can go back to get their glass. It's a big help in a big family."

- **Yard work**

    "Little ones love to pull weeds, and that's a good way to teach them the parts of the plant," Rosie said. "You see who can pull the plant from the root all the way up."

"One of their favorite things is piling leaves into the wagons or wheelbarrows and taking a ride in the barrow to the compost heap," she said. "We usually have two or three barrows, and the children have races."

Toddlers can water the lawn with a hose, too, Rosie said. "We let them take off their clothes. They get cooled off and play in the water, but do the watering at the same time."

- **Feeding pets and other animals**

"Andrea likes to help her older brothers and sister put out fresh water and pour dry food into the animals' dishes and bowls," Rosie said.

Use chore time to help you discover a child's natural bent

From the time children are preschoolers you can begin to observe the direction of their personalities and natural talents through chores. "Some are the more careless type, and others are more precise," Rose said. "The child who tears into the bathroom and leaves streaks of Ajax all over the sink and mirror is the one who is gifted at going outside and digging up a big hole two feet wide if you need it."

"Watch and see who they are," Rosie said. "It tends to come out in the area of chores."

Kids Writing

Jason and Chris were a couple of 14-year-old boys I taught in a home school co-op creative writing class one year. One day when I asked the class to take out their writing notebooks, both boys said they had left theirs in another room. I told them to go back to get the notebooks, and then...then I made the mistake of looking at my watch and saying I would time them.

Unfortunately, those fast-growing young giants hadn't quite figured out what to do with the extra inches they had recently acquired in their legs and feet. In the race to get back, while trying to make the turn into our classroom, they collided with each other and the wall. The door sign went flying along with their notebooks. Jason cut his eyebrow and scraped the side of his face so raw that I had to turn him over to one of the other co-op moms for first aid.

The boys expected me to scold them, but instead I told them, "Now you have something to write about. Describe what happened in your notebook."

It was a great opportunity to show the class that, for a writer, everything is grist for the mill. Anything that happens – or fails to happen – can stimulate a writing project.

When parents keep that in mind, too, they can stimulate their children to keep up essential writing skills during the summer. For children need to keep reading and writing during the long summer break to strengthen these skills and prevent their loss. Spending even 10 to 15 minutes a day reading and writing can pay big dividends over the course of the summer.

Writing is a 3-step process

Encouraging children to write is less overwhelming if you see it as a three-step process: brainstorming, writing, and editing.

In the brainstorming phase you talk through or scribble and list ideas to decide what you will write about. In writing, you let the words and ideas pour out. In editing, you work on the mechanics: re-write sentences, re-arrange ideas, correct spelling and grammar, etc.

Teachers spend a lot of time working with children on the editing process during the school year. Over the summer, parents can let that ride. The important thing is to encourage the flow of writing ideas, whether a trickle or a flood.

Don't try to write and edit at the same time

People (of all ages) get stuck when they try to write and edit at the same time. If they stop moving their pen in the middle of a piece to critique their idea arrangement or look up a spelling word, they lose the flow of their ideas. Their brains refuse to switch gears back and forth from writing to editing.

That's why I gave my junior high students rapid-writing exercises. I told them to write whatever came to mind, rolling along without stopping for ten minutes. If they felt it was hard, they could write about how hard they felt it was. If they couldn't think of a word, they could write "I can't think of the word" in place of the word and kept moving. This helped them learn to keep writing without stopping to edit.

To keep students from confusing writing flow with editing, I told them that the writing process is like sculpting. Brainstorming is like the process a sculptor goes through to decide on an idea. Rapid-writing is like gathering up and shaping a big batch of clay. Editing is like fussing with the details of the sculpture—poking, pinching, rearranging, throwing out chunks, attaching pieces, firing, glazing, etc.

How reading aloud to your kids helps their writing

Whatever children experience over the summer, whatever they

read themselves, and whatever parents read to them can all flow into writing practice. So read stories to children daily and encourage them to retell the stories to someone else in words or through art, puppetry, pantomime, etc.

Remember that children develop both reading and writing skills when they listen to stories that are written beyond their own reading level. Hearing good literature builds their vocabularies and establishes a strong sense of proper English and good writing style. This is why it is important for parents to keep reading aloud to children even into junior high.

Drawing can stimulate writing for some

Art stimulates the writing process for many children. So encourage them to make drawings and then write labels, captions, cartoon dialogue, or explanations. Whenever children start to get hung up on the mechanics of writing, like forming cursive script or spelling, suggest they draw instead.

After reading or hearing a story children can illustrate one or more scenes; make a cartoon strip showing the plot; draw a picture or map of the story's setting; invent and illustrate a new ending or invent and illustrate a new story using the same setting. Children can also use art to tell about their experiences through letter writing and journaling.

Tailor writing and art suggestions to the developmental level of your child

Art suggestions should be tailored to the age of the child. A preschooler might draw one scene from a story and tell you about it as you write down what he dictates. A sixth grader may be interested enough to draw the whole story scene by scene as a cartoon strip. (Show respect for their efforts by keeping their projects in a three ring binder.)

Encourage children to write (and draw) letters to relatives and friends describing daily activities and special events of the summer.

And keep a family journal or scrapbook, especially while on vacation. Talk with children about what they want to say in the letter or journal first (brainstorming) and encourage older children to jot down a list of their ideas first. Then let the writing flow.

Healthy Snacks

Parents and teachers often say that every child is different. Sometimes that's obvious—children come in different sizes, shapes, and shades. Other differences take more discernment to recognize—differences in personalities, learning styles, talents and abilities. But whatever their differences, children have one thing in common. They all seem to get hungry before supper.

Cookies and candy too close to mealtime may spoil a child's appetite for supper, but nutritious, sugarless snacks can settle nerves and arguments without undermining children's need for balanced nutrition.

Just before mealtime snack:

If children are ravenous during meal preparation, let them snack on the salad you plan to serve for supper, or else put out a big plate of fruit slices or raw vegetables—carrot, celery, and jicama sticks, broccoli, cauliflower, green pepper, or whatever you have available. It won't spoil their appetite, and they'll be taking the edge off their appetites with one of the most nutritious parts of the meal.

After-school snacks, parties and between meals snacks without sugar overload:

- **Kids' nachos:** Cover a cookie sheet with aluminum foil, then spread out one layer of tortilla chips, sprinkle with grated cheese (and salsa, if your children like it) and broil about one minute until the cheese is melted. If you have a microwave, you can put the chips on a plate and melt the cheese in the microwave instead. 30 seconds or one minute is usually enough time.
- **Popcorn:** Popcorn makes a good snack anytime. For a change, make a batch of popcorn and sprinkle it with Parmesan cheese.

- **Raw vegetables plus:** Fill celery sticks with cream cheese, peanut butter, or pimento cheese. Or make a dip for carrot and celery sticks, cucumbers, green pepper slices, broccoli and cauliflower flowerets, crackers or chips. For taco dip, mix two tablespoons of taco seasoning with 1 cup sour cream. For French onion dip, mix half an envelope of French onion soup with 1 cup sour cream. Veggies are good dipped in Ranch dressing, too.
- **Fruit and Cheese:** Apple and orange slices are always good, and so are chunks of cheese, with or without crackers. Kids like cheese chunks, grapes and other fruit speared with toothpicks for a special treat. Apple slices are yummy spread with peanut butter, too.
- **Blender treats:** Peel a banana, wrap in plastic wrap, and freeze. Blend frozen banana with ½ cup half-and-half, 2 tablespoons honey, and 1 teaspoon vanilla in an electric blender on high speed until smooth. Or blend a banana and a few frozen strawberries in 1 ½ cups of cold orange juice.
- **Frozen banana dip:** Slice bananas in half and insert an ice cream stick in the cut end. Freeze on a cookie sheet or in a pan and store in Ziplock bags. When you want to eat them, allow the bananas to thaw slightly and dip them into different toppings such as peanut butter, finely chopped nuts, flavored yogurt or coconut.
- **Nutty yogurt:** Stir ¼ cup Grape Nuts cereal or granola into an 8-ounce container of flavored yogurt.
- **Cracker sandwich:** Make a sandwich with a slice of cheese, smoked turkey luncheon meat and two rye crackers.
- **Cracker faces:** Spread crackers with peanut butter and make funny faces on the crackers with raisins, banana rounds, or apple chunks and slices.
- **Juicesicles and juice cubes:** Pour juice into an ice cube tray and freeze, to make juice cubes. Make popsicles by pouring fruit juice into paper cups. Place a plastic spoon in each cup and freeze. Peel off the paper to eat. Or you can buy plastic popsicle

molds at a grocery store.

- **Quick pizza snack:** Spread 2 tablespoons of spaghetti sauce on the halves of a split English muffin or bagel. Cover with pepperoni slices and grated mozzarella cheese. Broil 3 to 5 minutes (about 1 minute in the microwave) until the cheese melts.
- **Quesadillas:** Lightly oil and heat a large frying pan, place a tortilla (corn or flour) in the pan, sprinkle generously with grated cheese, and top with another tortilla. Cover and cook on low to medium heat until the cheese is melted. Flip with a spatula to brown the top tortilla lightly. Cut in four pie-shaped wedges and serve, with or without four dollops of picante sauce and sour cream on top.
- **Sausage balls:** Preheat oven to 350 degrees. Combine ½ pound thawed sausage (about room temperature) with 1 cup grated cheddar and 2 cups biscuit mix with your hands. Form into walnut-size balls and space them a few inches apart on an ungreased baking sheet. Bake 30 minutes. Makes about four dozen.

Science at Home

The science children read about in textbooks at school is easier for them to grasp when they are given lots of opportunities to experience hands on science at home and in the neighborhood. This is easier than most parents realize. Here are a few simple, hands on projects for any family:

- **Take a walk.**

    Notice the different shapes and fragrances of flowers, leaves, and bushes you pass. Check out ant hills and passing insects. Look under bushes to find nature's odds and ends (bird droppings, beetle shells, odd looking seeds), and try to figure out how each piece got there. An inexpensive magnifying glass or a pair of binoculars will add whole new dimensions of interest to your walks.

    Take a good look at buildings you pass, too. Notice unusual features and talk about different ways to build. Visit construction sites and notice the tools and machines men use to construct roads or buildings.

    Encourage any interest your child shows, avoiding pressure. Simply enjoy the discovery process together. If your child begins to ask a lot of questions, make a trip to the library together to try to find answers and books that tell more about the subjects that interest him.

- **Grow a kitchen garden.**

    The top inch of carrots, radishes, turnips or beets will grow leaves if you set the plant cut-side down in a shallow dish of water. Place the top inch of a pineapple in wet sand and transplant it to a pot with soil after a few weeks.

    A sweet potato (suspended small end down), a regular potato, or an avocado pit (suspended pointed end up) will grow into a beautiful plant if you insert three toothpicks into the pit or potato to hold it up in a jar of water. The potatoes need a sunny window to grow, but the avocado should be kept in a dark place until leafy shoots appear. Then plant it in soil.

Children can eat kitchen garden produce in a dinner salad if they sprout seeds. Almost any kind of natural (not chemically treated) seed can be sprouted except tomato seeds (which are poisonous when sprouted). Alfalfa, mung beans, lentils, and wheat kernels are easy to sprout and easy to obtain in a health food store.

Place the seeds in a wide mouthed jar with a piece of cheesecloth or clean nylon stocking stretched over the top and secured with a rubber band. Soak two or three tablespoons of seeds in water overnight. The next morning drain, rinse, and then drain them again. Continue rinsing and draining the seeds two or three times a day to keep the seeds moist but not wet.

Beans and peas are ready to harvest when they are 1-1/2 to 3 inches long. Except for alfalfa, grain sprouts are ready when they are as long as the seed. Alfalfa sprouts can grow until tiny green leaves appear. Sunflower and sesame seeds should be eaten as soon as they sprout, or else they develop a bitter taste.

- **Make an ant farm.**

Fit a glass or plastic container inside a larger, wide mouthed glass jar or plastic container so that there is a space ½ to 1 inch wide between the two containers. Fill that space with dirt, tamping gently, and then add a few ants. (You can eliminate the inside jar if you dig up a whole ant hill and pour it into a large glass container.)

Place a screen over the container mouth to give your ants air while preventing them from escaping. A piece of nylon stocking held in place with a rubber band works, too. Every few days add a bit of jam or a few cookie crumbs and honey or sugar water. In a week you should be seeing lots of tunnels and activity. After 10 days to two weeks, release the ants back outdoors.

- **Grow a crystal garden.**

Children can grow a weird, crystallized salt garden that changes by the hour and is fascinating to watch. Arrange porous materials like bark, cork, pieces of sponge, and lava rock in a jumbled mass in a shallow glass pan or aluminum pie plate.

Then mix up and spoon this solution over the pieces of porous material: 4 tablespoons non-iodized salt, 4 tablespoons liquid bluing (found with laundry products in the grocery store), 4 tablespoons water, and 1 tablespoon ammonia. Be sure the solution covers the bottom of the container, and drip one or two colors of food coloring over the garden.

Place the garden where you will not have to move it, and watch it turn into an eerie Martian landscape. It should grow for about four days, until the salt solution dries out.

(For more messy learning activities, see *Glorious Glop: save money and delight your kids with homemade art supplies, untidy science experiments, and other messy fun activities* in the Bookstore at www.beckypowers.com)

Lighten Up!

My 14-year-old son Matt and I were driving along the highway listening to the radio once when Ricky Nelson's recording "I'm a Travelin' Man" came on the oldies station.

As I listened to Nelson's musical brag about all the girl friends he "loved" and left behind in various parts of the world, I thought, *I can't just let this message go by with no comment.* I didn't want our son to absorb the idea that it's cool and manly to treat a woman like a sack lunch. On the other hand, I didn't want to turn him off by preaching a sermon.

Singing along with Ricky Nelson

So when Nelson started singing his chorus—*"Oh, I'm a Travelin' Man..."* I joined in with my own version of the chorus: *"Oh, I'm a Really Big Jerk..."*

Matt glanced at me sideways and grinned. "Yeah!" he agreed.

No lecture required.

A sense of humor can be a parent's best ally in the daily ups and downs of raising a family.

A short joke can get a parent's message across to children better than a long lecture and make the family feel closer, all at the same time. In addition, social worker Richard Park says, studies show that laughing together helps make people more objective about their problems, reduces their sensitivity to pain, and even increases their physical fitness. A 10-second belly laugh, Park says, has the same effect on the heart as 10 minutes of aerobic exercise.

Laughter in the family can be healthy or unhealthy, he added. Mockery and sarcasm are unhealthy kinds of laughter that poorly functioning families use to block intimacy. Healthy laughter is laughing with someone, not against someone.

Here are a few ways families can lighten up and laugh:

- **Back off, watch your children, and just enjoy them.**

    I remember the time our 4-year-old and his playmate visited the backyard playground in graduate student housing where we lived. Unknown to us, a repairman had dismantled the merry-go-round, and the two children showed up at the back door smeared with thick, black axle grease—arms, legs, hands, faces, necks...

    "Look, Mom!" Erik announced proudly. "We painted ourselves."

    The only thing to do was laugh and get out the camera. (Followed by a big bar of soap and the hose.)

- **Write down the funny things your children say and do.**

    Keep the record in one place. Later the family can have a lot of good laughs together reading about the past.

- **Look at photo albums together.**

    The pictures will bring up lots of laughs along with the memories.

- **Collect and share jokes.**

    Young children often enjoy reading joke books and retelling the jokes. Take time to listen and laugh. When people send me good jokes online, I print them out, three-hole punch them, and keep them in a binder. When I'm having a bad day, I page through the binder for a little perspective and share it with the family.

    And don't forget to share jokes soon after you hear them, along with the funny tapes and videos you discover. Once on a visit, our 12-year-old granddaughter discovered my joke binder and copied many of the jokes to make her own joke book. I also look for kids' jokes online and mail them to my far away grandchildren.

- **Remind yourself that it is OK to be silly.**

    "When things get too serious," Park says, "nonsense makes the most sense."

Use Rhymes to Teach Essentials

Like most native born Americans, I learned the English alphabet to the tune of "Twinkle Twinkle Little Star." I still recite it to the rhythm of that song when I am looking up names in the phone book:

" *ABCDEFG*
HIJKLMNOP
QRS and TUV
WX and Y and Z
Now I've said my ABC's
Say them with me if you please."

Children learn basic information better when they learn it through a song, a rhyme, or some kind of memorable saying.

Ditties to teach writing numerals

Here is a group of ditties (by my favorite author, Anonymous) for teaching preschoolers and first graders how to form their numbers.

1 - Straight down makes a one.
2 - Around and back/On the railroad track.
3 - Around and around once more.
4 - Down and over and down once more/
That's the way you make a four.
5 - Down and around, put a line on top.
6 - Down to a loop, and six rolls a hoop.
7 - Across the sky and down from heaven/
That's the way you make a seven.
8 - We make an "S" but we do not wait/
We climb back up to make an eight.
9 - A loop and a line makes nine.
10 - It's easy to make a ten: a one and an O/
You have ten fingers, you know.

Try introducing these sayings one at a time as you teach the numbers over several days, weeks, or months, depending on your child's interest (and need, if he or she is in first grade).

First, write the number yourself, reciting the saying as you write. It's best to start by writing it big, with a fat crayon on paper or with chalk on a blackboard or sidewalk. Next, write it in the air with big motions, repeating the ditty. Then have your child write it in the air a few times while reciting the saying together with you. Finally, let him or her write it with crayon or chalk, still reciting the ditty aloud. The next day, ask him to write it for you again in the air. Give him chances every day to do it again once or twice in different ways: writing in the air, writing in dirt or sand or cornmeal, writing with pencil, chalk, or marker.

Rhymes for teaching emergency information

By kindergarten, children need to learn their full name, their parents' names, and their address and phone number. It is a lot easier to teach them addresses and phone numbers if you make up a little rhyme and teach children the information in that form.

Here are a few samples:

Hemley Way in Vinton is the place I like to be
The number on my house is Eight Fifty-Three

In El Paso, Texas there's a little piece of heaven,
In a house on Third Street, number Ninety-Five Oh Seven.

My house in Anthony is on Stotts Avenue
Look and you will find number Eight Six Two.

Please please tell me that you'll be my valentine
Phone Eight Seven Seven Thirty Nine Twenty Nine

Roses are red, violets are blue
Five Eight Eight Sixty-Three Fifty-Two

Repeat these rhymes with your little ones when you are driving in the car or doing chores together. That way you will be keeping the information fresh in their minds, and they will be more apt to remember in case of an emergency.

Once in a while it's also a good idea to review the information in a different way by saying, "Let's pretend that you got lost and somebody said, 'What's your phone number?' What would you say?" That helps make your children familiar with the kinds of questions adults might ask them. And it helps them rehearse how to use the information they have memorized for a crisis.

Fun with Magnets

For children, magnets are fascinating toys with magical powers. For parents, magnets can be powerful teaching tools that introduce children to basic concepts about matter and energy. And fortunately, parents don't have to know a lot of science themselves to introduce children to magnets and have fun with them. They can enjoy discovering and learning along with their children.

A simple bar magnet or horseshoe magnet is all you need at first. For a stronger magnet, go to a farm supply store and ask for a cow magnet.

Explore the magnet's power

Start by letting children find out the magnet's power for picking up or moving things. Spread a number of small metal objects on a table – things you find easily around the house like pins and needles, thumb tacks, small nails and screws, coins, paper clips, scissors, rings and watches. Add in some non-metallic items, also. Encourage children to figure out for themselves what the magnet can or cannot attract, what it moves, and what it picks up. Talk with them about these discoveries as they make them.

Let them find out what happens when they stroke a needle or a thin nail several times in one direction across one end (or magnetic pole) of the magnet. This magnetizes the needle or the nail so that it attracts other metal objects. (Do not rub the needle back and forth over the pole; it only works if you stroke it several times in the same direction.) Show children that they can magnetize several paper clips so they attract one another and can form a chain.

Try simple experiments

Can a magnet attract a paper clip through air? Through water?

Paper? Cloth? Glass? To help children find out, try each of these experiments: Hold a magnet up in the air over a paper clip. Drop a paper clip into a dish of water with a magnet. Put a piece of paper over the magnet and move it toward a paper clip. Do the same with a piece of cloth. Place a paper clip in a thin drinking glass so that it rests against the side of the glass. See if you can make the paper clip move up the side of the glass using the magnet.

Make magnetic games

As you help children make these different discoveries over several days, you can also show them how to make a few magnetic games and toys that fascinate children of all ages. Just remember, for safety's sake, to keep small items like paper clips out of the hands of very small children.

- **Fishing game:** Cut fish shapes out of paper and attach a paper clip to the snout of each fish. Attach a length of string with tape to a kid-sized fishing pole (such as a yardstick or an empty gift wrap tube), and tie a small magnet to the end of the line. "Catch" fish with the magnet.
- **Variations:** use a cardboard box or a big cushion as a "boat" to fish from; fish against the clock; place the fish in a paper sack; fish with your eyes closed; cut your fish shapes from styrofoam trays instead of paper and float them in a tub of water.
- **Paper clip sculpture:** Magnetize a collection of paper clips using a strong bar magnet. Using the magnet as a base, try to make simple shapes like letters of the alphabet. You should be able to get the magnetized clips to connect with each other end-to-end, vertically and horizontally. Pinch the top piece of the shape gently with your fingers to keep the sculpture upright.
- **Magnetic sail boat:** Cut a small boat shape from a chunk of thick styrofoam. Make a sail from a piece of paper, using a darning needle or knitting needle for the mast. Poke the needle into the boat and float it in a small tub of water. Use the magnet to pull the boat around in the water.

- **Magnetic maze:** Draw a path on a piece of poster board or light cardboard. Small children can draw a squiggly line with a thick marking pen. Older kids may enjoy designing a maze. Whatever they create, they will then enjoy moving a paper clip along their pathway on top of the cardboard using a magnet underneath the cardboard. Pretend the paper clip is a fish looking for his supper or make up your own story.
- **Magnetic puppets:** On a piece of paper or light cardboard about four inches high, draw a figure on the top three inches. Fold the bottom inch under the figure to make a little stand. Clip a large paper clip to the stand. Then make a miniature theater from a light cardboard box or a decorated piece of poster board. Move your figure around using a magnet underneath the "ground" the puppet stands on.

Note: If you have trouble finding a large magnet (too big to be swallowed) for a preschooler, try ordering one from a store that specializes in educational materials for parents and teachers. Or buy magnetic tape with a self-stick backing from a craft store and make your own big magnet by sticking the tape onto a block of wood.

Teaching Jessica History

A few years ago, our daughter Jessica told me that a publisher had expressed interest in her new YA (young adult) novel project (*Amina: through my eyes*, by J.L. Powers), a story set in Somalia. The publisher wanted YA international historical fiction in modern wartime settings. Jessica set her story in Somalia because there is a large population of Somali refugees in the California Bay area where she was living that she could interview for background.

As she related her storyline, I felt a surge of *déjà vu* and by the time we hung up the phone, my mind was on a fast trot down memory lane. Jessica's first YA novel was set on the border of Mexico and Texas, her second YA novel was set in South Africa, and now she was working on one set in Somalia. *Her writing career is becoming a repeat of what we did in home school!* I thought: *Pick a time period, spin the globe, choose a spot, and start researching to write a story set in that time and place.*

We started homeschooling Jessica when she was 10 because she had lost her curiosity and her creative spark in public school, and because she was begging to be homeschooled like her little brother. Fortunately, at the outset of this adventure I read good advice about homeschooling a child burnt out on classroom-style learning: *plug into your child's passion*. Start where she finds delight, and from there guide her into broader fields of related study. Use the momentum of her delight in doing what she loves to help her climb the hard hills of subjects she dislikes.

Jessica's delights were writing, literature in general, and historical literature in particular. At 10, she read every book in Laura Ingalls Wilder's *Little House* series and decided she wanted to write books like Wilder. I scheduled our school days to complete academic schoolwork by noon and leave afternoons free for the kids to pursue their special interests. Jessica usually used her free time to read and write novels.

At the time, I was publishing parenting columns and family interest features in our local paper, the *El Paso Times*. That helped us both, I think. Jessica was reading my published work and hearing her friends' parents talk to me about things I'd written. Sometimes people would even talk to *her* about things I'd written. Those experiences made publication seem attainable (if Mom can publish, so can I someday), and it also made her take my writing suggestions more seriously.

The heroine in Jessica's first story was a young girl trying to help slaves escape through the Underground Railway. For a while, she became absorbed with the Civil War era, looking up encyclopedia entries and searching out biographies and novels set during that time period.

Then she read Corrie Ten Boom's *The Hiding Place* and became fascinated with World War II history. And so it went from 5th through 12th grade.

Jessica's passion for historical research and writing persuaded me to take a radical approach to her history studies. After our first year of homeschool, I jettisoned the use of history textbooks except as reference materials for Jessica's writing projects. From then on, her history courses consisted of reading historical novels, then researching and writing historical stories of her own. I figured that reading a wide variety of historical novels and stories was helping her develop a more vivid sense of various historical periods than she could acquire by reading textbooks. And trying to write historical fiction herself cemented the information in her mind. So Jessica would choose a historical era that fascinated her, and then we'd spin the globe and choose a place on earth for her to research as a basis for a story in that era.

I made no attempt to keep up with all the reading she did. I gave no tests or lectures. I just tried to be attentive and responsive—paying attention to Jessica's interests, listening, asking questions, sharing thoughts, affirming her work and ideas, making suggestions (usually offhand) and giving her tools for learning on her own. On our long walks we sometimes discussed her characters and plots. I was researching and writing a narrative nonfiction book myself at the time (although I could only work on it during summer breaks) so Jessica and I had a lot in common to share and discuss. I tried not to overwhelm her with writing critiques, although at times I'd say, "I'd let this go for most kids your age, but you are a really good writer, Honey. You can stretch and do even better. So I'd like you to think about this, that, or the other…"

When Jessica was 15, one year before she left for the university, I assigned a U.S. history textbook and a world history textbook for her to read to help fill in any missing gaps in her over-all knowledge of history and to give her a mental timeline for all the historical information she had acquired through reading and writing.

Then off she went to college, where she outgrew me as a mentor. That's one thing I've learned about mentoring. A good mentor gets outgrown. The mentee graduates to independence and after that, in the best of worlds, she becomes a colleague. Today I'm grateful for the invaluable help Jessica gives me with editing and marketing.

Education, Western Culture and the Bible

American kids need to know about the Bible, whether their families are religious or not, according to author and home school curriculum expert Ruth Beechick.

Without general Bible knowledge, children lack essential information to understand higher level reading material in English, she explained. They also lack the keys to assumptions that underlie broad subjects areas such as western history, politics, science and law. Even their understanding of our culture's art and music will be anemic without an understanding of the Bible.

Many, many literary references require readers to know Bible stories

Beechick described the research of E. D. Hirsh Jr., an English professor at the University of Virginia and author of *Cultural Literacy*. "(He said) that our literacy problem is not due to a lack of phonics," Beechick said. "It's due to a lack of knowledge people bring to their reading."

For example, when you read the phrase "David and Goliath" in the sports or business section of the newspaper, the "writers take for granted that you know of the little underdog challenging the giant," she said. A person who is unfamiliar with Bible stories will miss the writer's meaning.

"(Hirsh) and his associates did research on all kinds of common reading materials like newspapers and magazines." Beechick said. Then they catalogued all specific items like "David and Goliath" that writers take for granted people understand.

"The resulting dictionary includes 26 pages of Bible information, which is almost 5% of the total," Beechick said. "No other single book comes anywhere close to dominating as the Bible does. For instance, all other literature in English uses 30 pages of the dictionary, just a bit more than the Bible uses by itself."

Understanding western culture requires Bible knowledge

Bible knowledge is also necessary for understanding western culture. "The Bible is the basis of our western civilization in more ways than most people realize," Beechick said. "For one thing, it's the basis of our law."

Beechick explained that the law of the Hebrew people, written down in the Bible, was different from other ancient systems of law in two ways. First, the Hebrews believed that the source of their law was God, not their rulers. So from the Bible came the idea of equality and the rule of law – that leaders must obey the law just like everyone else.

Second, the Hebrews valued human life. "The main concern of Babylonian law (for example) was to protect property belonging to the upper echelons of society," Beechick said. "The main concern of Hebrew law was the sanctity of the individual, who (they believed) was formed in the image of God."

America's system of law and its political freedom are rooted in the Bible.

The Bible strongly influenced Roman law after the empire became Christian, Beechick said. American law is rooted in Roman civil law and in English common law, which was often developed by Christian clergy appointed as judges.

U.S. political freedom is also rooted in the Bible, she said. "The idea that man is important and has rights...caused people to struggle for their freedom, and it gradually led to the kind of freedom we have in the west."

"History is just not history if you leave out religion," Beechick went on. "If you leave out Christianity and Judaism and Islam, and really understanding those three religions all through western history, then you have an anemic history."

The history of scientific discovery is rooted in the Bible's teachings

Philosopher Alfred North Whitehead called Christianity the "mother of science," Beechick said, because "Copernicus believed that a creation by God would have rational design and thus would be knowable within human limits. These two ideas of design and knowability are critical in Western science."

Many of the "fathers" of modern science were Bible believers, Beechick said. A few of those she listed were Francis Bacon, father of the scientific method of empirical research; Robert Boyle, father of chemistry; Blaise Pascal, father of hydrostatics and analytic geometry; and Nicholas Steno, father of stratigraphy.

Art, music and literature are filled with themes from the Bible

"Bible themes appear extensively in art, music and literature," Beechick said. Students cannot fully understand these subject areas if they lack knowledge about the stories and the ideas referred to in western creative works.

Beechick quoted Hirsh and his researchers' conclusion: "No one in the English-speaking world can be considered literate without a basic knowledge of the Bible."

How can parents give children Bible knowledge?

Parents face a problem here because they cannot rely on public schools to give their children the Bible knowledge they need for a well-rounded education. The Bible is not normally taught in school because of a movement to remove religious influence from all state and federal institutions. So, if parents want their children to be well educated, they need to provide this part themselves.

The easiest way to start, Beechick said, is to buy and read children a good Bible story book. Actually, a Bible story book is a good place to start even for college students and adults. "Home school parents are finding out that they can get a best look at a topic, like astronomy for example, by reading something simple written for children first. They get a good overview that way."

Other suggestions: Read a modern translation of the Bible. Contact local churches and synagogues to find out about Bible classes for children and adults. For a wealth of artistically created videos online showing themes of the Bible and overviews of all the books in the Bible, go to https://bibleproject.com/

For videos of a storyteller telling all the stories of the Bible, go to www.bibletelling.org .This website also provides all the stories of the Bible by phone call, no internet or computer needed. Call 559-670-1877 and enter a Story Number (1,2,3...for full-length stories, or 1001, 1002, 1003...for 90-second stories) To control story play back, 0 = Skip to end of story, 2 = Reverse 30 seconds, 3 = Forward 30 seconds, and 8 = Pause. Entering 555 gives instructions and more information. Entering 777 gives an overview of the entire Bible story.

Tackle Problems Head-On

One year when our daughter Jessica was about 12, we took the family to play miniature golf during a visit to Grandma and Grandpa Cerling's in Iowa. Jessica made the worst score, and Grandma, seeing that her granddaughter was feeling bad, moved in to comfort her.

"Well, Honey," Grandma said, putting her arm around the girl, "we can't all be winners, but we can all..."

She paused and thought a moment.

I waited.

Finally, after a long thoughtful pause "....we can all be losers," Grandma ended lamely.

Jessica looked blank.

And I laughed all the way home. "We can't all be winners, but we can all be losers!" What a thing to say to your granddaughter!

But so, so true, as I came to think about it later.

Not only *can* we all be losers, but life being what it is, at one time or another we all *will* be losers. It's as inevitable as the cutting of wisdom teeth, the advent of gray hair and menopause.

As a parent and grandparent, I don't enjoy losing. But it has had its positive side. A friend once said to me, "Failure gives you the opportunity to teach your children the most valuable thing they could learn from you: what to do after you fail....Children need to know that you can redeem a failure, that you can screw up and then go back and make it right."

That woman was in counseling with her husband and children, working hard to put a marriage and home back together after a series of crises and failures.

"The most beautiful thing I've learned from my husband," she said, "is that you can fail in a way that you break the hearts of the people you love, so that you're tempted to think you can never face them again. It takes courage and prayer, but you can decide, 'This is the end of the loss right here. I'm not going to lose any more.'"

How do you do this? How do you recoup failure as a parent?

First, don't hide the mess. Look at it.

Every family has problems. It isn't the presence or absence of problems that shows whether or not a family is healthy, it's how people choose to respond to the problems that inevitably come.

A healthy family gives most of its energy to recognizing, acknowledging, and dealing with its problems. An unhealthy (dysfunctional) family pours most of its energy into keeping up appearances and denying the problems, minimizing them or running away from them.

The 12 Step program from Alcoholics Anonymous (for those who fail through alcoholism) can be modified to help anyone coping with any kind of failure. Here are 10 of those steps:

1) *We admitted we were powerless over alcohol (or our teen's rebellion, or my cancer, or our family's business failure) – that our lives had become unmanageable.*
2) *We came to believe that a Power greater than ourselves could restore us to sanity.*
3) *We made a decision to turn our will and our lives over to the care of God as we understood Him.*

Second, sort out your responsibilities.
Then take steps to admit blame and make amends.

You are only responsible for what you can control. If a wife has an affair, her husband can't control that decision. She is responsible for making that choice, or for unmaking it. There are other things affecting the marriage relationship that the husband can control, however. If he belittles his wife, if he neglects her, he is responsible for those words and actions.

Steps 4 through 10 deal with this step of taking responsibility:

4) We made a searching and fearless moral inventory of

ourselves.
5) *We admitted to God, to ourselves, and to another human being the exact nature of our wrongs.*
6) *We were entirely ready to have God remove all these defects of character.*
7) *We humbly asked Him to remove our shortcomings.*
8) *We made a list of all persons we had harmed and became willing to make amends to them all.*
9) *We made direct amends to such people whenever possible except when to do so would injure them or others.*
10) *We continued to take personal inventory, and when we were wrong, we promptly admitted it.*

Part of taking responsibility involves making yourself accountable to others, like a counselor or a support group.

My prayer for myself and my family has become this: Lord, give us the wisdom to recognize when we're in a mess, the honesty to admit it, the courage to face it, and the perseverance to clean it up. Amen.

Acknowledgements

Thanks to my old friend Ruth Mead for her wise and cheerful mentoring when I was just beginning the parenting journey. And to Karyn Henley for sharing insights from her workshops on playing with children. Thanks to Izzy Mora, family support coordinator for Parents Anonymous of El Paso, for explaining how to recognize and replace a controlling attitude with nurturing and patient training. Thanks to Gayle Seerden, coordinator of the El Paso ADD Support Group for answering my questions about parenting children with ADD. Thanks to Judy Rauch, MedPlus X-ray technician, for giving our son Matt and me an introduction to the world of X-ray technology when Matt cracked his metacarpal. Thanks to author and psychologist Dr. Kevin Leman for giving me his time for a phone interview about bedtime battles. Dr. Leman is the author of numerous books including *Making Children Mind Without Losing Yours, Have a New Kid by Friday,* and *What a Difference a Mom Makes.* Thanks to Ruth Beechick for approving my condensed description of her instant reading method. Thanks as well to Barbara Ardus, curator of the El Paso Museum of History in El Paso for taking time to explain how to make the most out of visit to a history museum with children. Thanks to my old friend Rosie Chavarria Jones for sharing her expertise on introducing toddlers to family chores. And thanks to our son Matt for acquainting me with the phonemic games in *Phonemic Awareness in Young Children* by Marilyn Jager Adams, Barbara R. Foorman, et. al.

About the Author

 Becky Cerling Powers is the author of *Laura's Children: the Hidden Story of a Chinese Orphanage*, and the editor and compiler of *My Roots Go Back to Loving*, a collection of faith-based family stories from El Pasoans. She is also a former parenting columnist for the *El Paso Times*, the *Clinton Herald* and the *El Paso Scene*. Becky is a veteran homeschool grandma who helped start the first home school support group in El Paso in 1984 when Texas parents were battling for the freedom to homeschool their children. She and her husband Dennis live in Vinton, Texas. They have been married 50 years and have three adult children and 13 grandchildren. She blogs at www.beckypowers.com and can be reached at becky@beckypowers.com

www.ingramcontent.com/pod-product-compliance
Lightning Source LLC
Chambersburg PA
CBHW032115090426
42743CB00007B/362